Matthew Arnold

Irish essays and others

Matthew Arnold

Irish essays and others

ISBN/EAN: 9783744731584

Printed in Europe, USA, Canada, Australia, Japan

Cover: Foto ©Thomas Meinert / pixelio.de

More available books at **www.hansebooks.com**

IRISH ESSAYS

AND OTHERS

BY

MATTHEW ARNOLD

LONDON
SMITH, ELDER, & CO., 15 WATERLOO PLACE
1882

All rights reserved

PREFACE.

THE ESSAYS which make the chief part of this volume have all appeared during the last year or two in well-known periodicals. The Prefaces which follow at the end were published in 1853 and 1854 as prefaces to my *Poems*, and have not been reprinted since. Some of the readers of my poetry have expressed a wish for their reappearance, and with that wish I here comply. Exactly as they stand, I should not have written them now; but perhaps they are none the worse on that account.

The three essays regarding Ireland which commence the present volume, and which give it its title, were received with no great favour when they appeared, and will probably be received with no great favour now. Practical politicians and men of the world are apt rather to resent the incursion of a man of letters into the field of politics; he is, in truth, not on his own ground there,

PREFACE.

and is in peculiar danger of talking at random. No one feels this more than I do. Nevertheless I have set in the front of this volume the essays on Irish affairs. If I am asked why, I should be disposed to answer that I am curious to know how they will look ten years hence, if anyone happens then to turn to them.

English people keep asking themselves what we ought to do about Ireland. The great contention of these essays is, that in order to attach Ireland to us solidly, English people have not only to *do* something different rom what they have done hitherto, they have also to *be* something different from what they have been hitherto. As a whole, as a community, they have to acquire a larger and sweeter temper, a larger and more lucid mind. And this is indeed no light task, yet it is the capital task now appointed to us, and our safety depends on our accomplishing it : to *be* something different, much more, even, than to *do* something different.

I have enquired how far the Irish Land Act seemed likely, to a fair and dispassionate observer, to attach Ireland to us, to prove *healing*. It was easy to see reasons for thinking beforehand that it would not prove healing.

Now that it is in operation, it is easy to see reasons for thinking so still. At the present moment one especial aspect of the matter can hardly fail to catch any clear-sighted man's attention. No one can deny that the Act seems likely to have a very large and far-reaching effect. But neither can it be denied, on the other hand, that leading Ministers declared their belief, which of course was entirely sincere, that the number of extortionate landlords in Ireland was inconsiderable, and that the general reduction of rents in Ireland would be inconsiderable. But it turns out that probably the general reduction of rents in Ireland, through the operation of the Land Courts fixing a judicial rent, will, on the contrary, be very considerable. Most certainly the inference of the people of Ireland will be that the number of extortionate landlords, also, was in fact very considerable. But this was just the contention of the people of Ireland. The Government, however, did not admit its truth, and instituted the Land Courts without expecting that they would bring about any radical and universal change. If, therefore, they do bring about such a change, what, even though the Irish tenants profit by it, will be their gratitude to the Government? They will say that the English Government has done them a service without intending it, and without understanding and acknowledging the justice of their case. But so strong was the justice of their case, they will say, that it victoriously established itself as soon as the English Government, not dreaming of any such result, gave them a tribunal for determining a fair rent.

It seems to me impossible not to see this, if one does not either shut one's eyes or turn them another way. We shall have brought about a radical change, we shall have established by law a divided ownership full of critical consequences, we shall have disturbed the accepted and ordinary constitutive characters of property,— and we shall get little or no gratitude for it ; we shall be said to have done it without intending it. Our measure is not likely, therefore, of itself to avail to win the affections of the Irish people to us and to heal their estrangement. Yet to make a radical change, without doing this, opens no good prospect for the future. To break down the landlords in Ireland, as we have already broken down the Protestant Church there, is merely to complete the destruction of the *modus vivendi* hitherto existing for society in that country; a most imperfect *modus vivendi* indeed, but the only one practically attained there up to this time as a substitute for anarchy. Simply to leave to the Irish people the free and entire disposal of their own affairs is recommended by some counsellors as the one safe solution of the Irish difficulty. But the safety of this solution depends upon the state and dispositions of the people to whom we apply it. May not a people be in such a state that Shakespeare's words hold true of it—

> . . . Your affections are
> A sick man's appetite, who desires most that
> Which would increase his evil?

And may it not be affirmed, that if ever those words seemed true of any people, they seem true of the Irish at this hour?

To heal the estrangement between Ireland and England is what is needed above all things, and I cannot say that the Land Act appears to me to have in itself the elements for healing it. Nor can I see the use of pretending to find them in it if they are not really there.

Nothing, indeed, could be more absurd than for irresponsible people to press seriously their fancy solutions, though they may properly enough throw them out, on a suitable occasion, for purposes of discussion and illustration. Nothing, moreover, is further from my thoughts, in what is here said, than to find fault with the responsible Government, which has to provide not a fancy solution for difficulties, but a solution which may be put in practice. I know that it was as impossible to go on governing Ireland by means of the landlords as by means of the Protestant Church. I am ready to admit that the Government, the power and *purchase* at their disposal being what it is, could not well but have had recourse to some such measure as the Land Act. I think, even, as I have said in the following pages, that the Land Act of the Government, with what it does and what it gives the power of doing, is probably quite capable of satisfying the Irish people as a Land Act, if a certain other indispensable condition is complied with. But this condition the Land Act will not of itself realise. The indispensable condition is, that England and English civilisation shall become more attractive; or, as I began by saying, that we should not only *do* to Ireland something different from what we have done hitherto, but should also *be* something different. On this need of a changed and more attractive power in English civilisation almost all the essays in the present volume, and not alone those dealing directly with Ireland, will be found to insist.

The barren logomachies of Plato's *Theatetus* are relieved by half a dozen immortal pages, and among them are those in which is described the helplessness of the philosopher in the ways of the world, the helplessness of the man of the world in a spiritual crisis. The philosopher Thales in the ditch had been an easy and a frequent subject for merriment; it was reserved for Plato to amuse himself with the practical politician and man of the world in a spiritual crisis. Mr. Jowett is uncommonly happy in his translation of Plato's account of the man of the world, at such a crisis, 'drawn into the upper air,' having to 'get himself out of his commonplaces to the consideration of government and of human happiness and misery in general,—what they are, and how a man is to attain the one and avoid the other.' 'Then, indeed,' says Plato, 'when that narrow, vain, little practical mind is called to account about all this, he gives the philosopher his revenge. For dizzied by the height at which he is hanging, whence he looks into space which is a strange experience to him, he being dismayed and lost and stammering out broken words is laughed at, not by Thracian handmaidens such as laughed at Thales, or by any other uneducated persons, for they have no eye for the situation, but by every man who has been brought up as a true freeman.'

Our practical politicians and men of the world, carried up by the course of time and change into a new air, and still ruefully trying there to gasp out their formulas, such as 'Freedom of contract,' or 'The Liberal party has emphatically condemned religious endowment,' or 'Our traditional, existing, social arrangements,' could not be better hit off. The man of the world, with his utter astonishment that the Irish tenants should stop the hunting, when the hunting 'caused the noble master of the hounds to spend among them ten thousand a year!' the man of the world, with his mournful and incessant cries of 'Revolution!' Yes, we are in a revolution; 'a revolution,' as the late Duke of Wellington said, 'by due course of law.' And one of the features of it is, that the Irish tenants prefer to stop the hunting of those whom they regard as a set of aliens encamped amongst them for sporting purposes, who have in the past treated them and spoken to them as if they were slaves, and who are disposed, many of them, to treat them and speak to them as if they were slaves still,—the Irish people had rather stop this hunting, than profit by an expenditure upon it to the tune of ten thousand a year. The man of the world has had and has one formula for attaching neighbours and tenants to us, and one only,—expenditure. And now he is 'drawn into upper air,' and has to hear such new and strange formulas as this, for example, of the most charming of French moralists:—*Pour gagner l'humanité, il faut lui plaire; pour lui plaire, il faut être aimable.* Or, if the man of the world can stand Holy Writ, let him hear the Psalmist:—'*Mansueti possidebunt terram*, the gentle shall possess the earth.'

Indeed we are at the end of a period, and always at the end of a period the word goes forth: 'Now is the judgment of this world.' The 'traditional, existing, social arrangements,' which satisfied before, satisfy no longer; the conventions and phrases, which once passed without question, are challenged. That saying of the saints comes to be fulfilled: *Peribit totum quod non est ex Deo ortum.*

Each people has its own periods of national life, with their own characters. The period which is now ending for England is that which began, when, after the sensuous tumult of the Renascence, Catholicism being discredited and gone, our serious nation desired, as had been foretold, 'to see one of the days of the Son of Man and did not see it'; but men said to them, *See here*, or *See there*, and they went after the blind guides and followed the false direction; and the actual civilisation of England and of America is the result. A civilisation with many virtues! but without lucidity of mind, and without largeness of temper. And now we English, at any rate, have to acquire them, and to learn the necessity for us 'to live,' as Emerson says, 'from a greater depth of being.' The sages and the saints alike have always preached this necessity; the so-called practical people and men of the world have always derided it. In the present collapse of their wisdom, we ought to find it less hard to rate their stock ideas and stock phrases, their claptrap and their catchwords, at their proper value, and to cast in our lot boldly with the sages and with the saints. *Sine ut mortui sepeliant mortuos suos, sed tu vade adnuntia regnum Dei.*

CONTENTS.

	PAGE
THE INCOMPATIBLES	1
AN UNREGARDED IRISH GRIEVANCE	82
ECCE, CONVERTIMUR AD GENTES . .	109
THE FUTURE OF LIBERALISM	140
A SPEECH AT ETON . . .	181
THE FRENCH PLAY IN LONDON	205
COPYRIGHT	244
PREFACES TO POEMS	281

MATTHEW
 ARNOLD
IRISH ESSAYS
 (1882)

THE INCOMPATIBLES.

I.

The Irish Land Bill has not yet, at the moment when I write this, made its appearance. No one is very eager, I suppose, to read more about the Irish Land Bill while we do not yet know what the Bill will be. Besides, and above all, no one under any circumstances, perhaps, can much care to read what an insignificant person, and one who has no special connexion with Ireland, may have to say about the grave and sad affairs of that country.

But even the most insignificant Englishman, and the least connected with Ireland and things Irish, has a deep concern, surely, in the present temper and action of the Irish people towards England, and must be impelled to seek for the real explanation of them. We find ourselves,—though conscious, as we assure one another, of nothing but goodwill to all the world,—we find ourselves the object of a glowing, fierce, unexplained hatred on the part of the Irish people. 'The Liberal Ministry resolved,' said one of our leading Liberal statesmen a few years ago, when the Irish Church Establishment was abolished, 'the Liberal Ministry resolved to knit the hearts of the empire into one harmonious concord, and knitted they were accordingly.' Knitted indeed! The Irish people send members to our Parliament, whose great recommendation with their constituencies is, says Miss Charlotte O'Brien, that they are wolves ready to fly at the throat of England; and more and more of these wolves, we are told, are likely to be sent over to us. These wolves ravin and destroy in the most savage and mortifying way; they obstruct our business, lacerate our good name, deface our dignity, make our cherished fashions of government impossible and ridiculous. And then come eloquent rhetoricians, startling us with the prediction that Ireland will have either to be governed in future despotically, or to be given up. Even more alarming are certain grave and serious observers, who will not leave us even the cold comfort of the rhetorician's alternative, but declare that Ireland is irresistibly drifting to a separation from us, and to an unhappy separation;—a separation which will bring confusion and misery to Ireland, danger to us.

For my part, I am entirely indisposed to believe the eloquent rhetoricians who tell us that Ireland must either be governed for the future as a Crown colony or must be given up. I am also entirely indisposed to believe the despondent observers who tell us that Ireland is fatally and irresistibly drifting to a separation, and a miserable separation, from England. I no more believe the eloquent rhetoricians than I should believe them if they prophesied to me that Scotland, Wales, or Cornwall would have either to be governed as Crown colonies for the future, or to be given up. I no more believe the despondent observers than I should believe them if they assured me that Scotland, Wales, or Cornwall were fatally and irresistibly drifting to a miserable separation from England. No doubt Ireland presents many and great difficulties, and England has many and great faults and shortcomings. But after all the English people, with 'its ancient and inbred piety, integrity, good nature, and good humour,' has considerable merits, and has done considerable things in the world. In presence of such terrifying predictions and assurances as those which I have been just quoting, it becomes right and necessary to say so. I refuse to believe that such a people is unequal to the task of blending Ireland with itself in the same way that Scotland, Wales, and Cornwall are blended with us, if it sets about the task seriously.

True, there are difficulties. One of the greatest is to

be found in our English habit of adopting a conventional account of things, satisfying our own minds with it, and then imagining that it will satisfy other people's minds also, and may really be relied on. Goethe, that sagest of critics, and moreover a great lover and admirer of England, noted this fault in us. 'It is good in the English,' says he, 'that they are always for being practical in their dealings with things; *aber sie sind Pedanten*,—but they are pedants.' The pedant is he who is governed by phrases and does not get to the reality of things. Elsewhere Goethe attributes this want of insight in the English, their acceptance of phrase and convention, and their trust in these,—their pedantry in short,—to the habits of our public life, and to the reign amongst us of party spirit and party formulas. Burke supplies a remarkable confirmation of this account of the matter, when he complains of Parliament as being a place where it is 'the business of a Minister still further to contract the narrowness of men's ideas, to confirm inveterate prejudices, to inflame vulgar passions, and to abet all sorts of popular absurdities.' The true explanation of any matter is therefore seldom come at by us, but we rest in that account of things which it suits our class, our party, our leaders, to adopt and to render current. We adopt a version of things because we choose, not because it really represents them ; and we expect it to hold good because we wish that it may.

But, 'it is not your fond desire or mine,' says Burke again, 'that can alter the nature of things; by contending against which, what have we got, or shall ever get, but defeat and shame?' These words of Burke should be laid to heart by us. We shall solve at last, I hope and believe, the difficulty which the state of Ireland presents to us. But we shall never solve it without first understanding it; and we shall never understand it while we pedantically accept whatever accounts of it happen to pass current with our class, or party, or leaders, and to be recommended by our fond desire and theirs. We must see the matter as it really stands; we must cease to ignore, and to try to set aside, the nature of things; 'by contending against which, what have we got, or shall ever get, but defeat and shame?'

Pedantry and conventionality, therefore, are dangerous when we are in difficulties; and our habits of class and party action, and our ways of public discussion, tend to encourage pedantry and conventionality in us. Now there are insignificant people, detached from classes and parties and their great movements, people unclassed and unconsidered, but who yet are lovers of their country, and lovers of the humane life and of civilisation, and therefore grievously distressed at the condition in which they see Ireland and Irish sentiment at the present time, and appalled at the prophecies they hear of the turn which things in Ireland must certainly take. Such persons,—who after all, perhaps, are not so very few in number,—may well desire to talk the case over one to another in their own quiet and simple way, without pedantry and conventionality, admitting unchallenged none of the phrases with which classes and parties are apt to settle matters, resolving to look things full in the face and let them stand for what they really are; in order that they may ascertain whether there is any chance of comfort in store, or whether things are really as black and hopeless as we are told. Let us perish in the light, at any rate (if perish we must), and not in a cloud of pedantry; let us look fairly into that incompatibility, alleged to be incurable, between us and the Irish nation.

Even to talk of the people inhabiting an island quite near to us, and which we have governed ever since the twelfth century, as a distinct nation from ourselves, ought to seem strange and absurd to us;—as strange and absurd as to talk of the people inhabiting Brittany as a distinct nation from the French. However, we know but too well that the Irish consider themselves a distinct nation from us, and that some of their leaders, upon this ground, claim for them a parliament, and even an army and navy and a diplomacy, separate and distinct from ours. And this, again, ought to seem as strange and absurd as for Scotland or Wales or Cornwall to claim a parliament, an army and navy, and a diplomacy, distinct from ours; or as for Brittany or Provence to claim a parliament, an army and navy, and a diplomacy, distinct from those of France. However, it is a fact that for Ireland such claims are made, while for Scotland, Wales, Cornwall, Brittany, and Provence, they are not. That is because Scotland, Wales, and Cornwall are really blended in national feeling with us, and Brittany and Provence with the rest of France. And it is well that people should come to understand and feel that it is quite incumbent on a nation to have its parts blended together in a common national feeling; and that there is insecurity, there is reason for mortification and humiliation, if they are not. At last this much, at least, has been borne in upon the mind of the general public in England, which for a long while troubled itself not at all about the matter,— that it is a ground of insecurity to us, and a cause of mortification and humiliation, that we have so completely failed to attach Ireland. I remember, when I was visiting schools in Alsace twenty years ago, I noticed a number of points in which questions of language and religion seemed to me likely to raise irritation against the French government, and to call forth in the people of Alsace the sense of their separate nationality. Yet all such irritating points were smoothed down by the power of a common national feeling with France; and we all know how deeply German and Protestant Alsace regretted, and still regrets, the loss of her connexion with France Celtic and Catholic. Undoubtedly this does great honour to French civilisation and to its attractive forces. We, on the other hand, Germanic and Protestant England, we have utterly failed to attach Celtic and Catholic Ireland, although our language prevails there, and although we have no great counter-nationality on the borders of Ireland to compete with us for the possession of her affections, as the French had Germany on the borders of Alsace.

England holds Ireland, say the Irish, by means of conquest and confiscation. But almost all countries have undergone conquest and confiscation; and almost all property, if we go back far enough, has its source in these violent proceedings. After such proceedings, however, people go about their daily business, gradually things settle down, there is well-being and tolerable justice, prescription arises, and nobody talks about conquest and confiscation any more. The Frankish conquest of France, the Norman conquest of England, came in this way, with time, to be no longer talked of, to be no longer even thought of.

The seizure of Strasburg by France is an event belonging to modern history. It was a violent and scandalous act. But it has long ago ceased to stir resentment in a single Alsatian bosom. On the other hand, the English conquest of Ireland took place little more than a century after the Norman conquest of England. But in Ireland it did not happen that people went about their daily business, that their condition improved, that things settled down, that the country became peaceful and prosperous, and that gradually all remembrance of conquest and confiscation died out. On the contrary, the conquest had again and again to be renewed; the sense of prescription, the true security of all property, never arose. The angry memory of conquest and confiscation, the ardour for revolt against them, have continued, therefore, to irritate and inflame men's minds. They irritate and inflame them still; the present relations between landlord and tenant in Ireland offer only too much proof of it.

But this is only saying over again that England has failed to attach Ireland. We must ask, then, what it is which makes things, after a conquest, settle peaceably down, what makes a sense of prescription arise, what makes property secure and blends the conquered people into one nation with the conquerors. Certainly we must put, as one of the first and chief causes, general well-being. Never mind how misery arises, whether by the fault of the conquered or by the fault of the conqueror, its very existence prevents the solid settlement of things, prevents the dying out of desires for revolt and change.

Now, let us consult the testimonies from Elizabeth's reign, when the middle age had ended and the modern age had begun, down to the present time. First we have this picture of Irish misery by the poet Spenser :—

Out of every corner of the woods and glens they came creeping forth upon their hands, for their legs could not bear them; they looked like anatomies of death, they spake like ghosts crying out of their graves; they did eat the dead carrions, happy where they could find them, yea, and one another soon after, insomuch as the very carcases they spared not to scrape out of their graves; and if they found a plot of water-cresses or shamrocks there, they flocked as to a feast for the time, yet not able long to continue these withal; that in short space there were none almost left.

Then, a hundred and forty years later, we have another picture of Irish misery, a picture drawn by the terrible hand of Swift. He describes 'the miserable dress and diet and dwelling of the people, the general desolation in most parts of the kingdom.' He says :—

Some persons of a desponding spirit are in great concern about the aged, diseased, or maimed poor ; but I am not in the least pain upon the matter, because it is very well known that they are every day dying and rotting by cold and famine, and filth and vermin, as fast as can be reasonably expected.

And again :—

I confess myself to be touched with a very sensible pleasure when I hear of a mortality in any country parish or village, where the wretches are forced to pay, for a filthy cabin and two ridges of potatoes, treble the worth ; brought up to steal or beg, for want of work ; to whom death would be the best thing to be wished for, on account both of themselves and the public.

Next and finally, after the lapse of a hundred and fifty years more, coming down to our own day, we have this sentence, strong and short, from Colonel Gordon :—

The state of our fellow-countrymen in the south-west of Ireland is worse than that of any people in the world,—let alone Europe.

I say, where there is this misery going on for centuries after a conquest, acquiescence in the conquest cannot take place ; a sense of permanent settlement and of the possessors' prescriptive title to their property cannot spring up, the conquered cannot blend themselves into one nation with their conquerors.

English opinion, indeed, attributes Irish misery to the faults of the Irish themselves, to their insubordination, to their idleness and improvidence, and to their Popish religion. But however the misery arises, there cannot, as I have already said, be fusion, there cannot be forgetfulness of past violences and confiscations, while the misery lasts. Still, if the misery is due to the faults of the Irish, it is in curing faults on their side that we have to seek the remedy, not in curing faults of our own.

Undoubtedly the native Irish have the faults which we commonly attribute to them. Undoubtedly those Anglo-Irish, who lead them, too often superadd to the passionate unreason of the natives our own domestic hardness and narrow doggedness, and the whole makes a very unpleasant mixture. Undoubtedly it is not agreeable to have people offering to fly like wolves at your throat,—these people knowing, at the same time, that you will not put out your full strength against them, and covering you on that account with all the more menace and contumely. England must often enough be disposed to answer such assailants gruffly, to vow that she will silence them once for all, and to ejaculate, as Cæsar did when he threatened to silence the tribune Metellus : 'And when I say this, young man, to say it is more trouble to me than to do it.' Were there ever people, indeed, who so aggravated their own difficulties as the Irish people, so increased the labour and sorrow of him who toils to find a remedy for their ills? 'Always ready to react against the despotism of fact,'—so their best friend [1] among their French kinsmen describes them. 'Poor brainsick creatures!'—a sterner critic [2] among these kinsmen says,—'poor brainsick creatures, distraught with misery and incurable ignorance! by inflaming themselves against the English connexion, by refusing to blend their blood, their habits, their hopes, with those of the leading country, they are preparing for themselves a more miserable future than that of any other people in Europe.' It seems as if this poor Celtic people were bent on making what one of its own poets has said of its heroes hold good for ever: 'They went forth to the war, *but they always fell.*'

All this may be very true. But still we ought to know whether the faults and misery of the Irish are due solely to themselves, and all we can do is to hold down the poor brainsick creatures and punish them,—which, to say the truth, we have done freely enough in the past; or whether their state is due, either in whole or in large part, to courses followed by ourselves, and not even yet

---

[1] M. Henri Martin.
[2] A writer in the *République Française.*

discontinued by us entirely, in which it may be possible to make a change.

Now, I imagine myself to be at present talking quietly to open-minded, unprejudiced, simple people, free from class spirit and party spirit, resolved to forswear self-delusion and make-believe, not to be pedants, but to see things as they really are. Such people will surely be most anxious, just as I too was anxious, on this question of the rights and the wrongs in England's dealings with Ireland, to put themselves in good hands. And if they find a guide whom they can thoroughly trust they will not be restive or perverse with him; they will admit his authority frankly. Now, Edmund Burke is here a guide whom we can thus trust. Burke is, it seems to me, the greatest of English statesmen in this sense, at any rate: that he is the only one who traces the reason of things in politics, and who enables us to trace it too. Compared with him, Fox is a brilliant and generous schoolboy, and Pitt is a schoolboy with a gift (such as even at school not unfrequently comes out) for direction and government. Burke was, moreover, a great *conservative* statesman,— conservative in the best sense. On the French Revolution his utterances are not entirely those of the Burke of the best time, of the Burke of the American War. He was abundantly wise in condemning the crudity and tyrannousness of the revolutionary spirit. Still, there has to be added to Burke's picture of the Revolution a side which he himself does not furnish; we ought to supplement him as we read him, and sometimes to correct him. But on Ireland, which he knew thoroughly, he was always the Burke of the best time; he never varied; his hatred of Jacobinism did not here make him go back one hair's breadth. 'I am of the same opinion,' he writes in 1797 (the year in which he died), 'to my last breath, which I entertained when my faculties were at the best.' Mr. John Morley's admirable biography has interested all of us afresh in Burke's life and genius; the Irish questions which now press upon us should make us seek out and read every essay, letter, and speech of Burke on the subject of Ireland.

Burke is clear in the opinion that down to the end of his life, at any rate, Irish misery and discontent have been due more to English misgovernment and injustice than to Irish faults. 'We found the people heretics and idolaters,' he says; 'we have, by way of improving their condition, rendered them slaves and beggars; they remain in all the misfortune of their old errors, and all the super-added misery of their recent punishment.' It is often alleged in England that the repeated confiscations of Irish lands and even the Popery Laws themselves, were necessitated by the rebelliousness and intractableness of the Irish themselves; the country could only be held down for England by a Protestant garrison, and through these severe means. Burke dissipates this flattering illusion. Even the Penal Code itself, he says, even 'the laws of that unparalleled code of oppression, were manifestly the effects of national hatred and scorn towards a conquered people, whom the victors delighted to trample upon, and were not at all afraid to provoke. *They were not the effect of their fears, but of their security.* They who carried on this system looked to the irresistible force of Great Britain for their support in their acts of power. They were quite certain that no complaints of the natives would be heard on this side of the water with any other sentiments than those of contempt and indignation. In England, the double name of the complainant, Irish and Papist (it would be hard to say which singly was the most odious), shut up the hearts of every one against them. They were looked upon as a race of bigoted savages, who were a disgrace to human nature itself.'

And therefore, although Burke declared that 'hitherto the p'an for the government of Ireland has been to sacrifice the civil prosperity of the nation to its religious improvement,' yet he declared, also, that '*it is injustice, and not a mistaken conscience,* that has been the principle of persecution.' That 'melancholy and invidious title,' he says, 'the melancholy and unpleasant title of grantees of confiscation, is a favourite.' The grantees do not even wish 'to let Time draw his oblivious veil over the unpleasant modes by which lordships and demesnes have been acquired in theirs and almost in all other countries upon earth.' On the contrary, 'they inform the public of Europe that their estates are made up of forfeitures and confiscations from the natives. They abandon all pretext of the general good of the community.' The Popery Laws were but part of a system for enabling the grantees of confiscation to hold Ireland without blending with the natives or reconciling them. The object of those laws, and their effect, was 'to reduce the Catholics of Ireland to a miserable populace, without property, without estimation, without education. They divided the nation into two distinct bodies, without common interest, sympathy, or connexion. One of these branches was to possess *all* the franchises, *all* the property, *all* the education ; the other was to be composed of drawers of water and cutters of turf for them.'

In short, the mass of the Irish people were kept without well-being and without justice. Now if well-being is a thing needed to make a conquered people one with its conquerors, so is justice, and so, also, is good treatment and kindness. Well might Burke adjure all concerned to 'reflect upon the possible consequences of keeping, in the heart of your country, a bank of discontent every hour accumulating, upon which every description of seditious men may draw at pleasure.' Well might he austerely answer that worthy Philistine at Bristol who remonstrated with them against making concessions to the Irish: 'Sir, it is proper to inform you that our measures *must be healing*.'[1] Well might he add: 'Their temper, too, must be managed, and their good affections cultivated.' Burke hated Jacobinism, the angry and premature destruction of the existing order of things, even more than he hated Protestant ascendency. But this, he remarked, led straight to the other. 'If men are kept as being no better than half citizens for any length of time, they will be made whole Jacobins.'

In 1797 this great man died, without having convinced Parliament or the nation of truths which he himself saw so clearly, and had seen all his life. In his very last years, while he was being hailed as the grand defender of thrones and altars, while George the Third thanked him for his 'Reflections on the French Revolution,' and while that book was lying on the table of every great house and every parsonage in England, Burke writes that as regards

[1] The italics are Burke's own.

Ireland he is absolutely without influence, and that, if any Irish official were known to share his views, such a man would probably be dismissed. What an illustration of the truth of Goethe's criticism on us: 'Their Parliamentary parties are great opposing forces which paralyse one another, and where the superior insight of an individual can hardly break through!'

Burke died three years before the Union. He left behind him two warnings, both of them full of truth, full of gravity. One is, that concessions, sufficient if given in good time and at a particular conjuncture of events, become insufficient if deferred. The other is, that concessions, extorted from embarrassment and fear, produce no gratitude, and allay no resentment. 'God forbid,' he cries, 'that our conduct should demonstrate to the world that Great Britain can in no instance whatsoever be brought to a sense of rational and equitable policy, but by coercion and force of arms.'

Burke thought, as every sane man must think, 'connexion between Great Britain and Ireland essential to the welfare of both.' He was for a Union. But he doubted whether the particular time of the closing years of the last century was favourable for a Union. Mr. Lecky, in his delightful book, *The Leaders of Public Opinion in Ireland*, expresses a like doubt. The restrictions on Irish trade had given to the Anglo-Irish and to the native Irish a joint interest, adverse to those restrictions; they had acted together in this interest, they had acted together on behalf of Irish independence ; the beginnings of a common national feeling between them had sprung up. The Catholics had been admitted to vote for members of Parliament, and it seemed likely that they would soon be declared capable of sitting in Parliament. But the Union came, and imported into the settlement of that matter a new personage, our terrible friend the British Philistine. And for thirty years this personage, of whose ideas George the Third was the faithful mouthpiece, delayed Catholic emancipation, which, without the Union, would probably have been granted much sooner. John Wesley wrote, Mr. Lecky tells us, against the withdrawal of the penal laws. At last, in 1829, the disabilities of Catholics were taken off, —but in dread of an insurrection. A wise man might at that moment well have recalled Burke's two warnings. What was done in 1829 could not have the sufficiency which in 1800 it might have had; what was yielded in dread of insurrection could not produce gratitude.

Meanwhile Irish misery went on ; there were loud complaints of the 'grantees of confiscation,' the landlords. Ministers replied, that the conduct of many landlords was deplorable, and that absenteeism was a great evil, but that nothing could be done against them, and that the sufferers must put their hopes in 'general sympathy.' The people pullulated in the warm stream of their misery; famine and Fenianism appeared. Great further concessions have since been made;—the abolition of tithes, the abolition of the Irish Church Establishment, the Land Act of 1870. But with respect to every one of them Burke's warnings hold good; they were given too late to produce the effect which they might have produced earlier, and they seemed to be given not from a desire to do justice, but from the apprehension of danger. Finally, we have to-day in parts of Ireland the misery to which Colonel Gordon bears witness; we have the wide-spread agitation respecting the land; we have the Irish people, if not yet 'whole Jacobins,' as Burke said we were making them, at least in a fair way to become so. And to meet these things we have coercion and the promised Land Bill.

For my part, I do not object, wherever I see disorder, to see coercion applied to it. And in Ireland there has been, and there is, most serious disorder. I do not agree with the orators of popular meetings, and I do not agree with some Liberals with whom I agree in general, I do not agree with them in objecting to apply coercion to Irish disorder, or to any other. Tumultuously doing what one likes is the ideal of the populace; it is not mine. True, concessions have often been wrung from governments only by the fear of tumults and disturbances, but it is an unsafe way of winning them, and concessions so won, as Burke has shown us, are never lucky. Unswerving firmness in repressing disorder is always a government's duty; so, too, is unswerving firmness in redressing injustice. It will be said that we have often governments firm enough in repressing disorder, who, after repressing it, leave injustice still unredressed. True; but it is our business to train ourselves, and to train public opinion, to make governments do otherwise, and do better. It is our business to bring them, not to be irresolute in repressing disorder, but to be both resolute in repressing disorder, and resolute, also, in redressing injustice.

'Sir, it is proper to inform you that our measures *must be healing.*' Ireland has had injustice and ill-treatment from us; measures are wanted which shall redress them and wipe out their memory. I do not yet know what the new Land Bill will be. But we have the Land Act of 1870 before our eyes, and we are told that proceeding a good deal further upon the lines of that Act is what is intended. Will this be *healing?*—that is the question. I confess that if one has no class or party interests to warp one, and if one is resolved not to be a pedant, but to look at things simply and naturally, it seems difficult to think so.

The truth is, as every one who is honest with himself must perceive,—the truth is, what is most needed, in dealing with the land in Ireland, is to redress our injustice, and to make the Irish see that we are doing so. And the most effective way, surely, to do this is not to confer boons on all tenants, but to execute justice on bad landlords. Property is sacred, will be the instant reply; the landlords, bad or good, have prescription in their favour. Property is sacred when it has prescription in its favour; but the very point is, that in Ireland prescription has never properly arisen. There has been such lack of well-being and justice there, that things have never passed,—at least they have never throughout the whole length and breadth of Ireland passed,—out of their first violent, confiscatory stage. 'I shall never praise either confiscations or counter-confiscations,' says Burke. A wise man will not approve the violences of a time of confiscation; but, if things settle down, he would never think of proposing counter-confiscation as an atonement for those violences. It is far better that things should settle down, and that the past should be forgotten. But in Ireland things have not settled down; and the harshness, vices, and neglect of many of the grantees of confiscation have been the main cause why they have not. 'The law bears, and must bear,' says Burke again, 'with the vices and follies of men, until they actually strike at the root of order.' In general, the vices and follies of individual owners of property are borne with, because they are scattered, single cases, and do not strike at the root of order. But in Ireland, they represent a system which has made peace and prosperity impossible, and which strikes at the root of order. Some good landlords there always were in Ireland; as a class they are said to be now good, certainly there are some who are excellent. But there are not a few, also, who are still very bad; and these keep alive in the Irish people the memory of old wrong, represent and continue to the Irish mind the old system. A government, by executing justice upon them, would declare that it breaks with that system, and founds a state of things in which the good owners of property, now endangered along with the bad, will be safe, in which a real sense of prescription can take root, in which general well-being and a general sense of good and just treatment,—that necessary condition precedent of Ireland's cheerful acquiescence in the English connexion,—may become possible, and the country can settle down. Such a measure would be a truly Conservative one, and every landowner who does his duty would find his security in it and ought to wish for it. A Commission should draw up a list of offenders, and an Act of Parliament should expropriate them without scruple.

English landowners start with horror at such a proposal; but the truth is, in considering these questions of property and land, *they are pedants.* They look without horror on the expropriation of the monastic orders by Henry the Eighth's Parliament, and many of them are at this very day great gainers by that transaction. Yet there is no reason at all why expropriating certain religious corporations, to give their lands to individuals, should not shock a man; but expropriating certain individual owners, to sell their lands in such manner as the State may think advisable, should shock him so greatly. The estates of religious corporations, as such, are not, says the conservative Burke severely but truly, 'in worse hands than estates to the like amount in the hands of this earl or that squire, although it may be true that so many dogs and horses are not kept by the religious.' But it was alleged that many monastic establishments, by their irregularities and vices, were a cause of public harm, struck at the root of order. The same thing may most certainly be said of too many Irish landlords at this day, with their harshness, vices, and neglect of duty. Reason of State may be alleged for dealing with both. In the mode of dealing, there can be no parallel. The monks were expropriated wholesale, good as well as bad, with little or no compensation. Of the landlords it is proposed to expropriate only the worst, so as to found for the good ones security and prescription; and the compensation assigned to the bad expropriated landlords by the English Parliament is sure to be not insufficient, rather it will be too ample.

For the confiscations of the lands of the native Irish themselves, from Elizabeth's time downwards, the plea of justification has been always this: *the reason of State*, the plea that the faults of the Irish possessor 'struck at the root of order.' Those confiscations were continuous and severe; they were carried on both by armed force and by legal chicane; they were in excess of what the reason of State, even at the time, seemed to fair men to require. 'By English Acts of Parliament,' says Burke, 'forced upon two reluctant kings, the lands of Ireland were put up to a mean and scandalous auction in every goldsmith's shop in London; or chopped to pieces and cut into rations, to pay the soldiery of Cromwell.' However, the justification was this, as I have said: the reason of State.

The faults of the Irish possessor struck at the root of order. And if order and happiness had arisen under the new possessors, not a word more would ever have been heard about past confiscations. But order and happiness have not arisen under them; a great part of the Irish people is in a chronic state of misery, discontent, and smouldering insurrection. To reconquer and chastise them is easy; but after you have chastised them, your eternal difficulty with them recommences. I pass by the suggestion that the Irish people should be entirely extirpated ; no one can make it seriously. They must be brought to order when they are disorderly; but they must be brought, also, to acquiescence in the English connexion by good and just treatment. Their acquiescence has been prevented by the vices, harshness, and neglect of the grantees of confiscation ; and it never will arise, so long as there are many of these who prevent it by their vices, harshness, and neglect still. Order will never strike root. The very same reason of State holds good, therefore, for expropriating bad landlords, which held good in their predecessors' eyes, and in the eyes of English Parliaments, for expropriating the native Irish possessors.

However, the expropriation of English or Anglo-Irish landlords is a thing from which English ministers will always avert their thoughts as long as they can, and another remedy for Irish discontent has been hit upon. It has been suggested, as every one knows, by the Ulster custom. In Ireland, the landlord has not been in the habit of doing for his farms what a landlord does for his farms in England; and this, too, undoubtedly sprang out of the old system of rule on the part of the grantees of confiscation as if they were lords and masters simply, and not men having a joint interest with the tenant. 'In Ireland,' says Burke, 'the farms have neither dwelling-houses nor good offices; nor are the lands almost anywhere provided with fences and communications. The landowner there never takes upon him, as it is usual in this kingdom, to supply all these conveniences, and to set down his tenant in what may be called a completely furnished farm. If the tenant will not do it, it is never done.' And if the tenant did it, what was done was still the property of the landlord, and the tenant lost the benefit of it by losing his farm. But in Ulster, where the tenants were a strong race and Protestants, there arose a custom of compensating them for their improvements, and letting them sell the value which by their improvements they had added to the property. But a bad landlord could set the custom at defiance; so the Land Act of 1870 regulated the custom, and gave the force of law to what had before possessed the force of custom only. And many people think that what ministers intend, is to develop considerably the principles and provisions of that Act,—so considerably, indeed, as to guarantee to the tenants fair rents, fixity of tenure, and free sale; and to extend the operation of the Act, so developed, to the whole of Ireland.

The new Bill is not yet before us; and I speak besides, as I well know and frankly avow, without special, local knowledge of Irish affairs. But a scheme such as that which has been indicated has inconveniences which must be manifest, surely, to every one who uses his common sense, and is not hindered from using it freely by the obligation not to do what would be really effective, but still to do something. Landowners hate parting with their land, it is true; but it may be doubted whether for the landlord to assign a portion of land in absolute property to the tenant, in recompense for the improvements hitherto effected, and in future himself to undertake necessary improvements, as an English landlord does, would not be a better, safer, and more pacifying solution of tenant-right claims, than either the Act of 1870, or any Act proceeding upon the lines there laid down. For it is evident that, by such an Act, ownership and tenure will be made quite a different thing in Ireland from that which they are in England, and in countries of our sort of civilisation generally; and this is surely a disadvantage. It is surely well to have plain, deep, common marks recognised everywhere, at least in all countries possessing a common civilisation, as characterising ownership and as characterising tenancy, and to introduce as little of novel and fanciful complication here as possible. Above all this is desirable, one would think, with a people like the Irish, sanguine and imaginative, who, if they are told that tenancy means with them more than it means elsewhere, will be prone to make it mean yet more than you intend. It is surely a disadvantage, again, to put a formal compulsion on good landlords to do what they were accustomed to do willingly, and to deprive them of all freedom and credit in the transaction. And the bad landlord, the real creator of our difficulties, remains on the spot still, but partially tied and entirely irritated; it will be strange indeed, if plenty of occasions of war do not still arise between him and his tenant, and prevent the growth of a sense of reconcilement, pacification, and prescription.

However, there are many people who put their faith in the Land Act of 1870, properly developed, and extended to the whole of Ireland. Other people, again, put their faith in emigration, as the means of relieving the distressed districts, and that, they say, is all that is wanted. And if these remedies, either the Land Act singly, or emigration singly, or both of them together, prove to be sufficient, there is not a word more to be said. If Ireland settles down, if its present state of smothered revolt ceases, if misery goes out and well-being comes in, if a sense of the prescriptive right of the legal owner of land springs up, and a sense of acquiescence in the English connexion, there is not a word more to be said. What abstracted people may devise in their study, or may say in their little companies when they come together, will not be regarded. Attention it will then, indeed, not require; and it is never easy to procure attention for it, even when it requires attention. English people live in classes and parties, English statesmen think of classes and parties in whatever they do. Burke himself, as I have said, on this question of Ireland which he had so made his own, Burke at the height of his fame, when men went to consult him, we are told, 'as an oracle of God,' Burke himself, detached from party and class, had no influence in directing Irish matters, could effect nothing. 'You have formed,' he writes to a friend in Ireland who was unwilling to believe this, 'you have formed to my person a flattering, yet in truth a very erroneous opinion of my power with those who direct the public measures. I never have been directly or indirectly consulted about anything that is done.'

No, *the English are pedants*, and will proceed in the ways of pedantry as long as they possibly can. They will not ask themselves what really meets the wants of a case, but they will ask what may be done without offending the prejudices of their classes and parties, and then they will agree to say to one another and to the world that this is what really meets the wants of the case, and that it is the only thing to be done. And ministers will always be prone to avoid facing difficulty seriously, and yet to do something and to put the best colour possible on that something; and so 'still further to contract,' as Burke says, 'the narrowness of men's ideas, to confirm inveterate prejudices, and to abet all sorts of popular absurdities.' But if a Land Act on the lines of that of 1870 fails to appease Ireland, or if emigration fails to prove a sufficient remedy, then quiet people who have accustomed themselves to consider the thing without pedantry and prejudice, may have the consolation of knowing that there is still something in reserve, still a resource which has not been tried, and which may be tried and may perhaps succeed. Not only do we not exceed our duty towards Ireland in trying this resource, if necessary, but, until we try it, we have not even gone to the extent of our duty. And when rhetoricians who seek to startle us, or despondent persons who seek to lighten their despondency by making us share it with them, when these come and tell us that in regard to Ireland we have only a choice between two desperate alternatives before us, or that we have nothing before us except ruin and confusion, then simple people, who have divested themselves of pedantry, may answer: 'You forget that there is one remedy which you have never mentioned, and apparently never thought of. It has not occurred to you to try breaking visibly, and by a striking and solemn act,—the expropriation of bad landlords,—with your evil and oppressive past in Ireland. Perhaps your other remedies may succeed if you add this remedy to them, even though without it they cannot.' And surely we insignificant people, in our retirement, may solace our minds with the imagination of right-minded and equitable Englishmen, men like the Lord Chief Justice of England, and Mr. Samuel Morley, and others whom one could easily name, acting as a Commission to draw up a list of the thoroughly bad landlords, representatives of the old evil system, and then bringing their list back to London and saying: 'Expropriate these, as the monks were expropriated, by Act of Parliament.' And since nothing is so exasperating as pedantry when people are in serious troubles, it may console the poor Irish, too, when official personages insist on assuring them that certain insufficient remedies are sufficient, and are also the only remedies possible, it may console them to know, that there are a number of quiet people, over here, who feel that this sort of thing is pedantry and make-believe, and who dislike and distrust our common use of it, and think it dangerous. These quiet people know that it must go on being used for a long time yet, but they condemn and disown it; and they do their best to prepare opinion for banishing it.

But the truth is, in regard to Ireland, the prejudices of our two most influential classes, the upper class and the middle class, tend always to make a compromise together, and to be tender to one another's weaknesses; and this is unfortunate for Ireland. It prevents the truth, on the two matters where English wrong-doing has been deepest,—the land and religion,—from being ever strongly spoken out and fairly acted upon, even by those who might naturally have been expected to go right in the matter in question. The English middle class, who have not the prejudices and passions of a landowning class, might have been expected to sympathise with the Irish in their ill-usage by the grantees of confiscation, and to interfere in order to relieve them from it. The English upper class, who have not the prejudices and passions of our middle class, might have been expected to sympathise with the Irish in the ill-treatment of their religion, and to interfere in order to relieve them from it. But nothing clouds men's minds and impairs their honesty like prejudice. Each class forbears to touch the other's prejudice too roughly, for fear of provoking a like rough treatment of its own. Our aristocratic class does not firmly protest against the unfair treatment of Irish Catholicism, because it is nervous about the land. Our middle class does not firmly insist on breaking with the old evil system of Irish landlordism, because it is nervous about Popery.

And even if the middle class were to insist on doing right with the land, it would be of no use, it would not reconcile Ireland, unless they can also be brought to do right, when the occasion comes, with religion. It is very important to keep this in full view. The land question is the question of the moment. Liberals are fond of saying that Mr. Gladstone's concessions will remove Irish discontent. Even the *Pall Mall Gazette*, the most serious and clear-minded of the exponents of Liberal ideas, talks sometimes as if a good Land Bill would settle everything. It will not; and it is deceiving ourselves to hope that it will. The thing is to bring Ireland to acquiesce cordially in the English connexion. This can be brought about only by doing perfect justice to Ireland, not in one particular matter only, but in all the matters where she has suffered great wrong. Miss O'Brien quotes an excellent saying of Fox's: 'We ought not to presume to legislate for a nation in whose feelings and affections, wants and interests, opinions and prejudices, we have no sympathy.' It is most true; and it is of general application. Mr. Bright is said to be desirous of dealing thoroughly with the Irish Land Question. With the wants and interests of the Irish people in this matter, even with their feelings and affections, opinions and prejudices, he is capable of sympathy. But how as to their wants and interests, feelings and affections, opinions and prejudices, in the matter of their religion? When they ask to have their Catholicism treated as Anglicanism is treated in England, and Presbyterianism is treated in Scotland, is Mr. Bright capable of sympathy with them? If he is, would he venture to show it if they made their request? I think one may pretty well anticipate what would happen. Mr. Carvell Williams would begin to stir, Mr. Jesse Collings would trot out that spavined, vicious-eyed Liberal hobby, expressly bred to do duty against the Irish Catholics: *The Liberal party has emphatically condemned religious endowment* ;—and I greatly fear that Mr. Bright would pat it approvingly.

'Sir, it is proper to inform you, that our measures *must be healing.*' Who but a pedant could imagine that our disestablishment of the Irish Church was a satisfaction of the equitable claims of Irish Catholicism upon us? that it was *healing*? By this policy, in 1868, 'the Liberal Ministry resolved to knit the hearts of the empire into one harmonious concord ; and knitted they were accordingly.' Parliament and public of pedants! they were nothing of the kind, and you know it. Ministers could disestablish the Irish Church, because there is among the Nonconformists of England and Scotland an antipathy to religious establishments; but justice to Irish Catholicism, and equal treatment with Anglicanism in England and with Presbyterianism in Scotland, your Government could not give, because of the bigotry of the English and Scotch of the middle class. Do you suppose that the Irish Catholics feel any particular gratitude to a Liberal Ministry for gratifying its Nonconformist supporters, and giving itself the air of achieving 'a grand and genial policy of conciliation,' without doing them real justice? They do not, and cannot ; and your measure was not healing. I think I was the only person who said so, in print at any rate, at the time. Plenty of people saw it, but *the English are pedants*, and it was thought that if we all agreed to call what we had done 'a grand and genial policy of conciliation,' perhaps it would pass for being so. But 'it is not your fond desire nor mine that can alter the nature of things.' At present I hear on all sides that the Irish

Catholics, who to do them justice are quick enough, see our 'grand and genial' act of 1868 in simply its true light, and are not grateful for it in the least.

Do I say that a Liberal Ministry could, in 1868, have done justice to Irish Catholicism, or that it could do justice to it now? 'Go to the Surrey Tabernacle,' say my Liberal friends to me; 'regard that forest of firm, serious, unintelligent faces uplifted towards Mr. Spurgeon, and then ask yourself what would be the effect produced on all that force of hard and narrow prejudice by a proposal of Mr. Gladstone to pay the Catholic priests in Ireland, or to give them money for their houses and churches, or to establish schools and universities suited to Catholics, as England has public schools and universities suited to Anglicans, and Scotland such as are suited to Presbyterians. What would be Mr. Gladstone's chance of carrying such a measure?' I know quite well, of course, that he would have no chance at all of carrying it. But the English people are improvable, I hope. Slowly this powerful race works its way out of its confining ruts and its clouded vision of things, to the manifestation of those great qualities which it has at bottom,—piety, integrity, good-nature, and good-humour. Our serious middle class, which has so turned a religion full of grace and truth into a religion full of hardness and misapprehension, is not doomed to lie in its present dark obstruction for ever, it is improvable. And we insignificant quiet people, as we had our consolation from perceiving what might yet be done about the land, when rhetoricians were startling us out of our senses, and despondent persons were telling us that there was no hope left, so we have our consolation, too, from perceiving what may yet be done about Catholicism. There is still something in reserve, still a resource which we have not yet tried, and which all classes and parties amongst us have agreed never to mention, but which in quiet circles, where pedantry is laid aside and things are allowed to be what they are, presents itself to our minds and is a great comfort to us. And the Irish too, when they are exasperated by the pedantry and unreality of the agreement, in England, to pass off as 'a great and genial policy of conciliation' what is nothing of the kind, may be more patient if they know that there is an increasing number of persons, over here, who abhor this make-believe and try to explode it, though keeping quite in the background at present, and seeking to work on men's minds quietly rather than to bustle in Parliament and at public meetings.

Before, then, we adopt the tremendous alternative of either governing Ireland as a Crown colony or casting her adrift, before we afflict ourselves with the despairing thought that Ireland is going inevitably to confusion and ruin, there is still something left for us. As we pleased ourselves with the imagination of Lord Coleridge and Mr. Samuel Morley, and other like men of truth and equity, going as a Commission to Ireland, and enabling us to break with the old evil system as to the land by expropriating the worst landlords, and as we were comforted by thinking that though this might be out of the question at present, yet perhaps, if everything else failed, it might be tried and succeed,—so we may do in regard to Catholicism. We may please ourselves with the imagination of Lord Coleridge and the other Mr. Morley,—Mr. John Morley,—and men of like freedom with them from bigotry and prejudice, going as a Commission to Ireland, and putting us in the right way to do justice to the religion of the mass of the Irish people, and to make amends for our abominable treatment of it under the long reign of the Penal Code,—a treatment much worse than Louis the Fourteenth's treatment of French Protestantism, much worse, even, than the planters' treatment of their slaves, and yet maintained without scruple by our religious people while they were invoking the vengeance of heaven on Louis the Fourteenth, and were turning up their eyes in anguish at the ill-usage of the distant negro. And here, too, though to carry a measure really *healing* may be out of the question at present, yet perhaps, if everything else fails, such a measure may at last be tried and succeed.

But it is not yet enough, even, that our measures should be healing. 'The temper, too, of the Irish must be managed, and their good affections cultivated.' If we want to bring the Irish to acquiesce cordially in the English connexion, it is not enough even to do justice and to make well-being general; we and our civilisation must also be attractive to them. And this opens a great question, on which I must proceed to say something.

II.

SINCE the foregoing remarks were written, the Irish Land Bill has been brought into Parliament. It is much what was anticipated. And it is easy enough, no doubt, to pick holes in the claim of such a measure to be called *healing*.

For let us recapitulate how the matter stands. It stands thus. The Irish chafe against the connexion with this country. They are exasperated with us; they are, we are told, like wolves ready to fly at the throat of England. And their quarrel with us, so far as it proceeds from causes which can be dealt with by a Land Act,—their quarrel with us is for maintaining the actual land-system and landlords of Ireland by the irresistible might of Great Britain. Now, the grievance which they allege against the land-system and landlords is twofold; it is both moral and material. The moral grievance is, that the system and the men represent a hateful history of conquest, confiscation, ill-usage, misgovernment, and tyranny. The material grievance is, that it never having been usual with the landowner in Ireland, as it is in England, to set down his tenant in what may be called a completely furnished farm, the Irish tenant had himself to do what was requisite; but when he had done it, it was the landlord's property, and the tenant lost the benefit of it by losing his farm.

As to the material grievance there is no dispute. As to the moral grievance, it is urged on our side that 'the confiscations, the public auctions, the private grants, the plantations, the transplantations, which animated,' says Burke, 'so many adventurers to Irish expeditions,' are things of the past, and of a distant past; that they are things which have happened in all countries, and have been forgiven and forgotten with the course of time. True; but in Ireland they have not been forgiven and forgotten. And a fair man will find himself brought to the conservative Burke's conclusion, that this is mainly due to the proceedings of the English in-comers, with whom their 'melancholy and invidious title' of grantees of confiscation was for so long time a favourite, and who so long looked upon the native Irish as a race of bigoted savages, to be treated with contempt and tyranny at their pleasure. Instead of putting these disagreeable facts out of sight, as we are so apt to do when we think and speak of the state of Ireland, we ought resolutely to keep them before us. 'Even the harsh laws against popery were the product,' says Burke, 'of contempt and tyranny, rather than of religious zeal. From what I have observed, it is pride, arrogance, and a spirit of domination, and not a bigoted spirit of religion, that has caused and kept up these oppressive statutes.' The memory of the original 'terrible confiscatory and exterminatory periods' was thus kept alive, and the country never settled down.

However, it is urged, again, that the possessors of the soil are now quite changed in spirit towards the native Irish, and changed in their way of acting towards them. It is urged that some good landlords there always were, and that now, as a class, they are good, while there are many of them who are excellent. But the memory of an odious and cruel past is not so easily blotted out. And there are still in Ireland landlords, both old and new, both large and small, who are very bad, and who by their hardness and oppressiveness, or by their contempt and neglect, keep awake the sense of ancient, intolerable wrong. So stands the case with the moral grievance; it exists, it has cause for existing, and it calls for remedy.

The best remedy, one would have thought, would be a direct one. The grievance is moral, and is best to be met and wiped out by a direct moral satisfaction. Every one who considers the thing fairly will see that the Irish have a moral grievance, that it is the chief source of their restlessness and resentment, that by indirect satisfactions it is not easy to touch it, but that by such an act as the expropriation of bad landlords it would have been met directly. Such an act would be a moral expiation and satisfaction for a moral wrong; it would be a visible breaking, on the part of this country and its Government, with the odious and oppressive system long upheld by their power. The vices and follies of the bad landlords in Ireland have struck at the root of order. Things have gone on without real and searching cure there, until the country is in a revolutionary state. Expropriation is, say objectors, a revolutionary measure. But when a country is in a revolutionary state you must sometimes have the courage to apply revolutionary measures. The revolution is there already; you must have the courage to apply the measures which really cope with it. Coercion, imprisonment of men without trial, is a revolutionary measure. But it may be very right to apply coercion to a country in Ireland's present state; perhaps even to apply a coercion far more stringent and effectual than that which we apply now. It would be a revolutionary measure to have the bad landlords of Ireland scheduled in three classes by a Commission, and, taking twenty-five years' purchase as the ordinary selling-price of an Irish estate, to expropriate the least bad of the three classes of scheduled landlords at twenty years' purchase, the next class at fifteen years' purchase, the worst at ten years' purchase. But it would be an act justified by the revolutionary state into which the misdoing of landlords of this sort, preventing prescription and a secure settlement of things from arising, has brought Ireland. It would fall upon those who represent the ill-doers of the past, and who are actually ill-doers themselves. And finally, it would be a moral reparation and satisfaction, made for a great and passionately felt moral wrong, and would, as such, undoubtedly have its full effect upon the heart and imagination of the Irish people. To have commuted the partial ownership, which the Irish tenant has in equity acquired by his improvements of the land cultivated by him, for absolute ownership of a certain portion of the land, as Stein commuted the peasant's partial ownership in Prussia; to have given facilities, as is now proposed, for emigration, and for the purchase of land and its distribution amongst a greater number of proprietors than at present;—this, joined to the expropriation of bad landlords, is what might naturally occur to one as the simple and direct way of remedying Irish agrarian discontent, and as likely to have been effective and sufficient for the purpose.

The Land Bill of the Government has provisions for furthering emigration, and provisions to facilitate the purchase of land. But the moral grievance of the Irish occupier it does not deal with at all; it gives no satisfaction to it and attempts to give none. It directs itself exclusively to his material grievance. It makes no distinction between good and bad landlords,—it treats them all as alike. But to the partial ownership which the occupier has in equity acquired in the land by his improvements, it gives the force of law, establishes a tribunal for regulating and enforcing it, and does its best to make this sort of partial ownership perpetual. The desirable thing, if it could but be done, is, on the contrary, as every one who weighs the matter calmly must surely admit, to sweep away this partial ownership,—to sweep away tenant-right altogether. It is said that tenant-right is an Irish invention, a remedy by which the Irish people themselves have in some degree met the wants of their own case, and that it is dear to them on that account. In legislating for them we ought studiously to adopt, we are told, their inventions, and not to impose upon them ours. Such reasoners forget that tenant-right was a mere palliative, used in a state of things where thorough relief was out of the question. Tenant-right was better than nothing, but ownership is better still. The absolute ownership of a part, by a process of commutation like Stein's in Prussia, engages a man's affections far more than any tenant-right, or divided and disputable ownership in a whole. Such absolute ownership was out of the question when the Irish occupier invented tenant-right; but it would in itself please him better than tenant-right, and commutation might have now given it to him.

The Land Bill, on the other hand, adopts, legalises, formulates tenant-right, a description of ownership unfamiliar to countries of our sort of civilisation, and very inconvenient. It establishes it throughout Ireland, and, by a scheme which is a miracle of intricacy and complication, it invites the most contentious and litigious people in the world to try conclusions with their landlords as to the ownership divided between them.

I cannot think such a measure naturally healing. A divided ownership of this kind will probably, however, no more be able to establish itself permanently in Ireland than it has established itself in France or Prussia. One has the comfort of thinking that the many and new proprietors who will, it is to be hoped, be called into being by the Purchase Clauses, will indubitably find the plan of divided ownership intolerable, and will sooner or later get rid of it.

I had recourse to Burke in the early part of these

remarks, and I wish to keep him with me, as far as possible, to the end. Burke writes to Windham: 'Our politics want directness and simplicity. A spirit of chicane predominates in all that is done; we proceed more like lawyers than statesmen. All our misfortunes have arisen from this intricacy and ambiguity of our politics.' It is wonderful how great men agree. For really Burke is here telling us, in another way, only what we found Goethe telling when we began to discuss these Irish matters: *the English are pedants.* The pedant, the man of routine, loves the movement and bustle of politics, but by no means wants to have to rummage and plough up his mind; he shrinks from simplicity, therefore, he abhors it;

simplicity cannot be had without thinking, without considerable searchings of spirit. He abhors simplicity, and therefore of course his governments do not often give it to him. He has his formula, his catchword, which saves him from thinking, and which he is always ready to apply; and anything simple is, from its very simplicity, more likely to give him an opening to apply his formula. If you propose to him the expropriation of bad landlords, he has his formula ready, that *the Englishman has a respect for the eighth commandment.* If you propose to him to do justice to the Irish Catholics, he has his formula, at one time, that *the sovereign must not violate his corona-*

tion oath, at another, that *the Protestants of Great Britain are implacably hostile to the endowment of Catholicism in any shape or form,* or else, that *the Liberal party has emphatically condemned religious endowment.* A complicated intricate measure is the very thing for governments to offer him, because, while it gives him the gratifying sense of taking in hand something considerable, it does not bring him face to face with a principle, does not provoke him to the exhibition of one of those formulas which, in presence of a principle, he has always at hand in order to save himself the trouble of thinking. And having this personage to deal with, governments are not much to be blamed, perhaps, for approaching their object in an indirect manner, for eschewing simplicity and for choosing complication.

The Irish Land Bill, then, does not meet the moral grievance of the Irish occupier at all, and it meets his material grievance in a roundabout, complicated manner, and by means that are somewhat hard upon good landlords. But it does meet it after a fashion. And, in meeting it, it does not challenge the exhibition of any of the pedantic Englishman's stock formulas; while it effects, at the same time, some very useful things by the way.

And, certainly, governments which seek to compass their

ends in this kind of manner do not incur that severe condemnation which Burke passes upon ministers who make it their business 'still further to contract the narrowness of men's ideas, to confirm inveterate prejudices, to inflame vulgar passions, and to abet all sorts of popular absurdities.' No, not by any means do they deserve this formidable blame. But when Burke writes to the Duke of Richmond of that day, that, without censuring his political friends, he must say that he perceives in them no regular or steady endeavour of any kind to bestow the same pains which they bestow on carrying a measure, or winning an election, or keeping up family interest in a county, 'on that which is the end and object of all elections, namely, *the disposing our people to a better sense of their condition,*'—when Burke says this, then he says what does touch, it seems to me, both the present government, and almost all governments which come and go in this country;—touches them very nearly. Governments acquiesce too easily in the mass of us English people being, as Goethe says, pedants; they are too apprehensive of coming into conflict with our pedantry; they show too much respect to its formulas and catchwords. They make no regular or sustained endeavours of any kind to dispose us poor creatures to a better sense of our condition. If they acquiesce so submissively in our being pedants in politics, pedants we shall always be. We want guidance from those who are placed in a condition to see. 'God and nature never made them,' says Burke of all the pedantic rank and file of us in politics, 'to think or to act without guidance or direction.' But we hardly ever get it from our government.

And I suppose it was despair at this sort of thing, in his own time and commonwealth, which made Socrates say, when he was reproached for standing aloof from politics, that in his own opinion, by taking the line he did, he was the only true politician of men then living. Socrates saw that the thing most needful was '*to dispose the people to a better sense of their condition,*' and that the actual politicians never did it. And serious people at the present day may well be inclined, though they have no Socrates to help them, at any rate to stand aside, as he did, from the movement of our prominent politicians and journalists, and of the rank and file who appear to follow, but who really do oftenest direct them;—to stand aside, and to try whether they cannot bring *themselves*, at all events, to a better sense of their own condition and of the condition of the people and things around them.

The problem is, to get Ireland to acquiesce in the English connexion as cordially as Scotland, Wales, or Cornwall acquiesce in it. We quiet people pretend to no lights which are not at the disposal of all the world. Possibly, if we were mixed up in the game of politics, we should play it much as other people do, according to the laws of that routine. Meanwhile, not playing it, and being in the safe and easy position of lookers-on and critics, we ought assuredly to be very careful to treat the practical endeavours and plans of other people without pedantry and without prejudice, only remembering that our one business is to see things as they really are. Ireland, then, is to be brought, if possible, to acquiesce cordially in the English connexion; and to this end our measures must be *healing*. Now, the Land Bill of the Government does not seem to deserve thoroughly the name of a *healing* measure. We have given our reasons for thinking so. But the question is, whether that Bill proposes so defective a settlement as to make, of itself, Ireland's cordial acquiescence in the English connexion impossible, and to compel us to resign ourselves a prey to the alarmists. One cannot without unfairness and exaggeration say this of it. It is offered with the best intentions, it deals with the material grievance of the Irish occupier if not with his moral grievance, and it proposes to do certain unquestionably good and useful things, besides redressing this grievance. It will not of itself make the Irish acquiesce cordially in the English connexion. But then neither would a thoroughly good Land Bill suffice to do this. The partisans of the Government are fond of saying, indeed: 'A good Land Bill will take the political bread out of Mr. Parnell's mouth.' Mr. Parnell maintains, that he and his friends 'have the forces of nature, the forces of nationality, and the forces of patriotism,' working for the separation of Ireland from England: and so they have, up to the present time. Now, a good Land Bill will not suffice to stay and annul the working of these forces, though politicians who are busy over a Land Bill will always be prone to talk as if it would suffice to do whatever may be required. But it will not. Much more than a good Land Bill is necessary in order to annul the forces which are working for separation. The best Land Bill will not reduce to impotence the partisans of separation, unless other things are accomplished too. On the other hand, the present Land Bill is not so defective as that it need prevent cordial union, if these other things are accomplished.

One of them has been mentioned already in the former part of these remarks. I mean the equitable treatment of Catholicism. To many of the Liberal party it is a great deal easier to offer to Ireland a fair Land Bill, than to offer to her a fair treatment of Catholicism. You may offer as fair a Land Bill as you please ; but nevertheless if, presently, when the Irish ask to have public schools and universities suited to Catholics, as England has public schools and universities suited to Anglicans, and Scotland such as are suited to Presbyterians, you fall back in embarrassment upon your formula of pedants, *The Liberal party has emphatically condemned religious endowment,* then you give to the advocates of separation a new lease of power and influence. You enable them still to keep saying with truth, that they have 'the forces of nature, the forces of nationality, and the forces of patriotism,' on their side. ' Our measures *must be healing,*' and it is not only as to Irish land that healing measures are necessary ; they are necessary as to the Irish people's religion also.

If this were in any good measure accomplished, if, even, we offered the Land Bill which Mr. Gladstone brings forward now, and if we offered a treatment of Catholicism as well intentioned and as fair in its way, then indeed things would have a look of cheerful promise, and politicians would probably think that the grand consummation had been reached, and that the millennium was going to begin. But a quiet bystander might still be cool-headed enough to suspect, that for winning and attaching a people so alienated from us as the Irish, something more, even, is required than fair measures in redress of actual mis-usage and wrong. 'Their temper, too, must be managed, and their good affections cultivated.'

Many of us talk as if the mere calculation of their interest, of the advantage to their commerce, industry, and security from the English connexion, must induce the Irish to blend readily with us, if they were but treated justly. But with a people such as the Irish, and when once such a feeling of repulsion has been excited in them as we have managed to excite, the mere redress of injustice and the calculation of their interest is not alone sufficient to win them. They must find in us something that in general suits them and attracts them; they must feel an attractive force, drawing and binding them to us, in what is called our civilisation. This is what blends Scotland and Wales with us; not alone their interest, but that our civilisation in general suits them and they like it. This is what so strongly attached to France the Germanic Alsace, and keeps it attached in spirit to France still: the wonderfully attractive power of French civilisation.

Some say, that what we have in Ireland is a lower civilisation, hating the advent of a higher civilisation from England, and rebelling against it. And it is quite true, that certain obvious merits of the English, and by which they have much prospered,—such as their exactness and neatness, for instance (to say no more than what everybody must admit),—are disagreeable to Irish laxity and slovenliness, and are resisted by them. Still, a high civilisation is naturally attractive. The turn and habits of the French have much that is irksome and provoking to Germans, yet French civilisation attracted Alsace powerfully. It behoves us to make quite sure, before we talk of Ireland's lower civilisation resisting the higher civilisation of England, that our civilisation is really high,—high enough to exercise attraction.

Business is civilisation, think many of us; it creates and implies it. The general diffusion of material well-being is civilisation, thought Mr. Cobden, as that eminent man's biographer has just informed us; it creates and implies it. Not always. And for fear we should forget what business and what material well-being have to create, before they do really imply civilisation, let us, at the risk of being thought tiresome, repeat here what we have said often of old. Business and material well-being are signs of expansion and parts of it; but civilisation, that great and complex force, includes much more than even that power of expansion of which they are parts. It includes also the power of conduct, the power of intellect and knowledge, the power of beauty, the power of social life and manners. To the building up of human life all these powers belong. If business is civilisation, then business must manage to evolve all these powers; if a widely spread material well-being is civilisation, then that well-being must manage to evolve all of them. It is written: *Man doth not live by bread alone.*

Now, one of the above-mentioned factors of civilisation is, without doubt, singularly absent from ours,—the power of social life and manners. 'The English are just, but not amiable,' was a sentence which, as we know, even those who had benefited by our rule felt themselves moved to pass on us. We underrate the strength of this particular element of civilisation, underrate its attractive influence, its power. *Mansueti possidebunt terram;*—the gentle shall possess the earth. We are apt to account amiability weak and hardness strong. But, even if it were so, 'there are forces,' as George Sand says truly and beautifully, 'there are forces of weakness, of docility, of attractiveness, or of suavity, which are quite as real as the forces of vigour, of encroachment, of violence, or of brutality.' And to those softer but not less real forces the Irish people are peculiarly susceptible. They are full of sentiment. They have by nature excellent manners themselves, and they feel the charm of manners instinctively.

'Courtesy,' says Vauvenargues, 'is the bond of all

society, and there is no society which can last without it.' But if courtesy is required to cement society, no wonder the Irish are estranged from us. For we must remember who it is of us that they mostly see, who and what it is that in the main represent our civilisation to them. The power of social life and manners, so far as we have it, is in Great Britain displayed above all in our aristocratic class. Mr. Carlyle's tribute to the manners and merits of this class will be fresh in our minds. 'With due limitation of the grossly worthless, I should vote at present that, of classes known to me in England, the aristocracy (with its perfection of human politeness, its continual grace of bearing and of acting, steadfast "honour," light address, and cheery stoicism), if you see well into it, is actually yet the best of English classes.' But our aristocracy, who have, on Mr. Carlyle's showing, this power of manners so attractive to the Irish nature, and who in England fill so large a place, and do really produce so much effect upon people's minds and imaginations, the Irish see almost nothing of. Their members who are connected with Ireland are generally absentees. Mr. Lecky is disposed to regret very much this want in Ireland of a resident aristocracy, and says that the Irish people are by nature profoundly aristocratical. At any rate, the Irish people are capable of feeling strongly the attraction of the power of manners in an aristocracy; and, with an aristocracy filling the place there which it fills in Great Britain, Ireland would no doubt have been something very different from what it is now.

While I admit, however, the merits of our aristocracy, while I admit the effect it produces in England and the important place it fills, while I admit that if a good body of it were resident in Ireland we should probably have Ireland in another and a more settled state, yet I do not think that a real solution would have been thus reached there any more than it has been reached, I think, here. I mean, if Ireland had had the same social system as we have, she would have been different from her present self indeed, but sooner or later she would have found herself confronting the same difficulty which we in England are beginning to feel now: the difficulty, namely, that the social system in question ends by landing modern communities in the possessorship of an upper class materialised, a middle class vulgarised, a lower class brutalised. But I am not going to discuss these matters now. What I want now to point out is, that the Irish do not much come across our aristocracy, exhibiting that factor of civilisation, the power of manners, which has undoubtedly a strong attraction for them. What they do come across, and what gives them the idea they have of our civilisation and of its promise, is our middle class.

I have said so much about this class at divers times, and what I have said about it has made me so many enemies, that I prefer to take the words of anybody rather than myself for showing the impression which this class is likely to make, and which it does make, upon the Irish, and the sort of idea which the Irish and others may be apt to form of the attractions of its civilisation for themselves, or for mankind in general, or for any one except us natives of Great Britain. There is a book familiar to us all, and the more familiar now, probably, to many of us, because Mr. Gladstone solaced himself with it after his illness, and so set all good Liberals (of whom I wish to be considered one) upon reading it over again. I mean *David Copperfield*. Much as I have published, I do not think it has ever yet happened to me to comment in print upon any production of Charles Dickens. What a pleasure to have the opportunity of praising a work so sound, a work so rich in merit, as *David Copperfield!* 'Man lese nicht die mit-strebende, mit-wirkende!' says Goethe: 'do not read your fellow-strivers, your fellow-workers!' Of the contemporary rubbish which is shot so plentifully all around us, we can, indeed, hardly read too little. But to contemporary work so good as *David Copperfield*, we are in danger of perhaps not paying respect enough, of reading it (for who could help reading it?) too hastily, and then putting it aside for something else and forgetting it. What treasures of gaiety, invention, life, are in that book! what alertness and resource! what a soul of good nature and kindness governing the whole! Such is the admirable work which I am now going to call in evidence.

Intimately, indeed, did Dickens know the middle class; he was bone of its bone and flesh of its flesh. Intimately he knew its bringing up. With the hand of a master he has drawn for us a type of the teachers and trainers of its youth, a type of its places of education. Mr. Creakle and Salem House are immortal. The type itself, it is to be hoped, will perish; but the drawing of it which Dickens has given cannot die. Mr. Creakle, the stout gentleman with a bunch of watch-chain and seals, in an arm chair, with the fiery face and the thick veins in his forehead; Mr. Creakle sitting at his breakfast with the cane, and a newspaper, and the buttered toast before him, will sit on, like Theseus, for ever. For ever will last the recollection of Salem House, and of 'the daily strife and struggle' there; the recollection 'of the frosty mornings when we were rung out of bed, and the cold, cold smell of the dark nights when we were rung into bed again; of the evening schoolroom dimly lighted and indifferently warmed, and the morning schoolroom which was nothing but a great shivering machine; of the alternation of boiled beef with roast beef, and boiled mutton with roast mutton; of clods of bread and butter, dog's-eared lesson-books, cracked slates, tear-blotted copy-books, canings, rulerings, hair-cuttings, rainy Sundays, suet-puddings, and a dirty atmosphere of ink surrounding all.'

A man of much knowledge and much intelligence, Mr. Baring Gould, published not long ago a book about Germany, in which he adduced testimony which, in a curious manner, proves how true and to the life this picture of Salem House and of Mr. Creakle is. The public schools of Germany come to be spoken of in that book, and the training which the whole middle class of Germans gets in them; and Mr. Gould mentions what is reported by young Germans trained in their own German schools, who have afterwards served as teachers of foreign languages and ushers in the ordinary private schools for the middle class in England. With one voice they tell us of establishments like Salem House and principals like Mr. Creakle. They are astonished, disgusted. They cannot understand how such things can be, and how a great and well-to-do class can be content with such an ignoble bringing up. But so things are, and they report their experience of them, and their experience brings before us, over and over again, Mr. Creakle and Salem House.

A critic in the *World* newspaper says, what is very true, that in this country the middle class has no naturally defined limits, that it is difficult to say who properly belong to it and who do not, and that the term, *middle class*, is taken in different senses by different people. This is most true. And therefore, for my part, to prevent ambiguity and confusion, I always have adopted an educational test, and by the middle class I understand those who are brought up at establishments which are more or less like Salem House, and by educators who are more or less like Mr. Creakle. And the great mass of the middle part of our community, the part which comes between those who labour with their hands, on the one side, and people of fortune, on the other, is brought up at establishments of the kind, although there is a certain portion broken off at the top which is educated at better. But the great mass are both badly taught, and are also brought up on a lower plane than is right, brought up ignobly. And this deteriorates their standard of life, their civilisation.

True, they have at the same time great merits, of which they are fully conscious themselves, and of which all who are in any way akin to them, and disposed to judge them fairly and kindly, cannot but be conscious also.

True, too, there are exceptions to the common rule among the establishments and educators that bring them up; there are good schools and good schoolmasters scattered among them. True, moreover, amongst the thousands who undergo Salem House and Mr. Creakle there are some born lovers of the humane life, who emerge from the training with natures unscathed, or who at any rate recover from it. But, on the mass, the training produces with fatal sureness the effect of lowering their standard of life and impairing their civilisation. It helps to produce in them, and it perpetuates, a defective type of religion, a narrow range of intellect and knowledge, a stunted sense of beauty, a low standard of manners.

And this is what those who are not akin to them, who are not at all disposed to be friendly observers of them, this is what such people see in them;—this, and nothing more. This is what the Celtic and Catholic Irish see in them. The Scotch, the Scotch of the Lowlands, of by far the most populous and powerful part of Scotland, are men of just the same stock as ourselves, they breed the same sort of middle class as we do, and naturally do not see their own faults. Wales is Celtic, but the Welsh have adopted with ardour our middle-class religion, and this at once puts them in sympathy with our middle-class

F

civilisation. With the Irish it is different. English civilisation means to the Irish the civilisation of our middle class; and few indeed are the attractions which to the Irish, with their quickness, sentiment, fine manners, and indisposition to be pleased with things English, that civilisation seems, or can seem, to have. They do not see the exceptions in our middle class; they do not see the good which is present even in the mis-trained mass of it. All its members seem of one type of civilisation to an Irish eye, and that type a repulsive one. They are all tarred with one brush, and that brush is Creakle's.

We may even go further still in our use of that charming and instructive book, the *History of David Copperfield*. We may lay our finger there on the very types in adult life which are the natural product of Salem House and of Mr. Creakle; the very types of our middle class, nay of Englishmen and the English nature in general, as to the Irish imagination they appear. We have only to recall, on the one hand, Mr. Murdstone. Mr. Murdstone may be called the natural product of a course of Salem House and of Mr. Creakle, acting upon hard, stern, and narrow natures. Let us recall, then, Mr. Murdstone; Mr. Murdstone with his firmness and severity, with his austere religion and his tremendous visage in church; with his view of the world as 'a place for action, and not for moping and droning in ;' his view of young Copperfield's disposition as 'requiring a great deal of correcting, and to which no greater service can be done than to force it to conform to the ways of the working world, and to bend it and break it.' We may recall, too, Miss Murdstone, his sister, with the same religion, the same tremendous visage in church, the same firmness; Miss Murdstone with her 'hard steel purse,' and her 'uncompromising hard black boxes with her initials on the lids in hard black nails;' severe and formidable like her brother, 'whom she greatly resembled in face and voice.' These two people, with their hardness, their narrowness, their want of consideration for other people's-feelings, their inability to enter into them, are just the type of the Englishman and his civilisation as he presents himself to the Irish mind by his serious side. His energy, firmness, industry, religion, exhibit themselves with these unpleasant features; his bad qualities exhibit themselves without mitigation or relief.

Now, a disposition to hardness is perhaps the special fault and danger of our English race in general, going along with our merits of energy and honesty. It is apt even to appear in all kinds and classes of us, when the circumstances are such as to call it forth. One can understand Cromwell himself, whom we earnest English

Liberals reverentially name 'the great Puritan leader,' standing before the Irish imagination as a glorified Murdstone ; and the late Lord Leitrim, again, as an aristocratical Murdstone. Mr. Bence Jones, again, improver and benefactor as he undoubtedly is, yet takes a tone with the Irish which may not unnaturally, perhaps, affect them much as Murdstone's tone affected little Copperfield. But the genuine, unmitigated Murdstone is the common middle-class Englishman, who has come forth from Salem House and Mr. Creakle. He is seen in full force, of course, in the Protestant north ; but throughout Ireland he is a prominent figure of the English garrison. Him the Irish see, see him only too much and too often. And he represents to them the promise of English civilisation on its serious side ; what this civilisation accomplishes for that great middle part of the community towards which the masses below are to look up and to ascend, what it invites those who blend themselves with us to become and to be.

The thing has no power of attraction. The Irish quick-wittedness, sentiment, keen feeling for social life and manners, demand something which this hard and imperfect civilisation cannot give them. Its social form seems to them unpleasant, its energy and industry to lead to no happiness, its religion to be false and repulsive. A friend of mine who lately had to pursue his avocations in Lancashire, in the parts about St. Helens, and who has lately been transferred to the west of Ireland, writes to me that he finds with astonishment, how 'even in the farthest *ultima Thule* of the west, amongst literally the most abjectly poverty-stricken cottiers, life appears to be more enjoyed than by a Lancashire factory-hand and family who are in the receipt of five pounds a week, father, mother, and children together, from the mill.' He writes that he finds 'all the country people here so full of courtesy and graciousness!' That is just why our civilisation has no attractions for them. So far as it is possessed by any great body in our own community, and capable of being imparted to any great body in another community, our civilisation has no courtesy and graciousness, it has no enjoyment of life, it has the curse of hardness upon it.

The penalty nature makes us pay for hardness is dulness. If we are hard, our life becomes dull and dismal. Our hardness grows at last weary of itself. In Ireland, where we have been so hard, this has been strikingly exemplified. Again and again, upon the English conqueror in his hardness and harshness, the ways and nature of the downtrodden, hated, despised Irish, came to exercise a strange, an irresistible magnetism. 'Is it possible,' asks Eudoxus, in Spenser's *View of the State of Ireland*, 'is it possible that an Englishman, brought up in such sweet civility as England affords, should find such liking in that barbarous rudeness that he should forget his own nature and forgo his own nation?' And Spenser, speaking under the name of Irenæus, answers that unhappily it did, indeed, often happen so. The Protestant Archbishop Boulter tells us, in like manner, that under the iron sway of the penal laws against Popery, and in the time of their severest exercise, the conversions from Protestantism to Popery were nevertheless a good deal more numerous than the conversions from Popery to Protestantism. Such, I say, is nature's penalty upon hardness. Hardness grows irksome to its very own self, it ends by wearying those who have it. If our hardness is capable of wearying ourselves, can we wonder that a civilisation stamped with it has no attractions for the Irish; that Murdstone, the product of Salem House and of Mr. Creakle, is a type of humanity which repels them, and that they do not at all wish to be like him?

But in Murdstone we see English middle-class civilisation by its severe and serious side only. That civilisation has undoubtedly also its gayer and lighter side. And this gayer and lighter side, as well as the other, we shall find, wonderful to relate, in that all-containing treasure-house of ours, the *History of David Copperfield.*

Mr. Quinion, with his gaiety, his chaff, his rough coat, his incessant smoking, his brandy and water, is the jovial, genial man of our middle-class civilisation, prepared by Salem House and Mr. Creakle, as Mr. Murdstone is its severe man. Quinion, we are told in our *History*, was the manager of Murdstone's business, and he is truly his pendant. He is the answer of our middle-class civilisation to the demand in man for beauty and enjoyment, as Murdstone is its answer to the demand for temper and manners. But to a quick, sentimental race, Quinion can be hardly more attractive than Murdstone. Quinion produces our towns considered as seats of pleasure, as Murdstone produces them considered as seats of business and religion. As it is Murdstone, the serious man, whose view of life and demands on life have made our *Hell-holes*, as Cobbett calls our manufacturing towns, have made the dissidence of dissent and the Protestantism of the Protestant religion, and the refusal to let Irish Catholics have schools and universities suited to them because their religion is *a lie and heathenish superstition*, so it is Quinion, the jovial man, whose view of life and demands on it have made our popular songs, comedy, art, pleasure, —made the City Companies and their feasts, made the London streets, made the Griffin. Nay, Quinion has been busy in Dublin too, for have we not conquered Ireland?

The streets and buildings of Dublin are full of traces of him; his sense of beauty governed the erection of Dublin Castle itself. As the civilisation of the French middle class is the maker of the streets and buildings of modern Paris, so the civilisation of the English middle class is the maker of the streets and buildings of modern London and Dublin.

Once more. Logic and lucidity in the organising and administering of public business are attractive to many; they are satisfactions to that instinct of intelligence in man which is one of the great powers in his civilisation. The immense, homogeneous, and (comparatively with ours) clear-thinking French middle class prides itself on logic and lucidity in its public business. In our public business logic and lucidity are conspicuous by their absence. Our public business is governed by the wants of our middle class, and is in the hands of public men who anxiously watch those wants. Now, our middle class cares for liberty; it does not care for logic and lucidity. Murdstone and Quinion do not care for logic and lucidity. Salem House and Mr. Creakle have not prepared them for it. Accordingly, we see the proceedings of our chief seat of public business, the House of Commons, governed by rules of which one may, I hope, at least say, without risk of being committed for contempt, that logic and lucidity have nothing to do with them. Mr. Chamberlain, again, was telling us only the other day, that 'England, the greatest commercial nation in the world, has in its bankruptcy law the worst commercial legislation of any civilised country.' To be sure, Mr. Chamberlain has also said, that 'if in England we fall behind other nations in the intelligent appreciation of art, we minister to a hundred wants of which the other nations have no suspicion.' As we are a commercial people, one would have thought that logic and lucidity in commercial legislation was one of these wants to which we minister; however, it seems that we do not. But, outside our own immediate circle, logic and lucidity are felt by many people to be attractive; they inspire respect, their absence provokes ridicule. It is a plea for Home Rule if we inflict the privation of them, in public concerns, upon people of quicker minds, who would by nature be disposed to relish them. Probably the Irish themselves, though they are gainers by the thing, yet laugh in their sleeves at the pedantries and formalities with which our love of liberty, Murdstone and Quinion's love of liberty, and our total want of instinct for logic and lucidity, embarrass our attempts to coerce them. Certainly they must have laughed outright, being people with a keen sense of the ridiculous, when in the information to which the traversers had to plead at the late trials, it was set forth that the traversers 'did conspire, combine, confederate, and agree together, to solicit, incite, and procure,' and so on. We must be Englishmen, countrymen of Murdstone and Quinion, loving liberty and a 'freedom broadening slowly down from precedent to precedent,'—not fastidious about modern and rational forms of speech, about logic and lucidity, or much comprehending how other people can be fastidious about them,—to take such a jargon with proper seriousness.

The dislike of Ireland for England the resistance of a lower civilisation to a higher one! Why, everywhere the attractions of this middle-class civilisation of ours, which is what we have really to offer in the way of civilisation, seem to fail of their effect. 'The puzzle seems to be,' says the *Times* mournfully, 'where we are to look for our friends.' But there is no great puzzle in the matter if we will consider it without pedantry. Our civilisation, as it looks to outsiders, and in so far as it is a thing broadly communicable, seems to consist very much in the Murdstonian drive in business and the Murdstonian religion, on the one hand, and in the Quinionian joviality and geniality, on the other. Wherever we go, we put forward Murdstone and Quinion, and call their ways civilisation. Our governing class nervously watch the ways and wishes of Murdstone and Quinion, and back up their civilisation all they can. But do what we will, this civilisation does not prove attractive.

The English in South Africa 'will all be commercial gentlemen,' says Lady Barker,—commercial gentlemen like Murdstone and Quinion. Their wives will be the ladies of commercial gentlemen, they will not even tend poultry. The English in the Transvaal, we hear again, contain a wonderful proportion of attorneys, speculators, land-jobbers, and persons whose antecedents will not well bear inspection. Their recent antecedents we will not meddle with, but one thing is certain : their early antecedents were those of the English middle class in general, those of Murdstone and Quinion. They have almost all, we may be very sure, passed through the halls of a Salem House and the hands of a Mr. Creakle. They have the stamp of either Murdstone or Quinion. Indeed we are so prolific, so enterprising, so world-covering, and our middle class and its civilisation so entirely take the lead wherever we go, that there is now, one may say, a kind of odour of Salem House all round the globe. It is almost inevitable that Mr. Sprigg should have been reared in some such establishment; it is ten to one that Mr. Berry is an old pupil of Mr. Creakle. And when they visit Europe, no doubt they go and see Mr. Creakle, where he is passing the evening of his days in honourable retirement,—a

Middlesex magistrate, a philanthropist, and a member of the Society of Arts. And Mr. Berry can tell his old master of a happy country all peopled by ourselves, where the Murdstone and Quinion civilisation seems to men the most natural thing in the world and the only right civilisation, and where it gives entire satisfaction. But poor Mr. Sprigg has to report of a land plagued with a large intermixture of foreigners, to whom our unique middle-class civilisation does not seem attractive at all, but they find it entirely disagreeable. And so, too, to come back much nearer home, do the Irish.

So that if we, who are in consternation at the dismal prophecies we hear concerning what is in store for Ireland and England, if we determine, as I say, to perish in the light at any rate, to abjure all self-deception, and to see things as they really are, we shall see that our civilisation, in its present state, will not help us much with the Irish. Now, even though we gave them really healing measures, yet still, estranged as the Irish at present are, it would be further necessary to manage their tempers and cultivate their good affections by the gift of a common civilisation congenial to them. But our civilisation is not congenial to them. To talk of it, therefore, as a substitute for perfectly healing measures is ridiculous. Indeed, the pedantry, bigotry, and narrowness of our middle class, which disfigure the civilisation we have to offer, are also the chief obstacle to our offering measures perfectly healing. And the conclusion is, that our middle class and its civilisation require to be transformed. With all their merits, which I have not here much insisted upon, because the question was, how their demerits make them to be judged by unfriendly observers,—with all their merits, they require, as I have so often said, to be transformed. And for my part I see no way so promising for setting about it as the abolishment of Salem House and of Mr. Creakle. This initiatory stage governs for them in a great degree all the rest, and with this initiatory stage we should above all deal.

I think I hear people saying : *There! he has got on his old hobby again!* Really, people ought rather to commend the strictly and humbly practical character of my writings. It was very well for Mr. Carlyle to bid us have recourse, in our doubts and miseries, to earnestness and reality, and veracity and the everlasting yea, and generalities of that kind; Mr. Carlyle was a man of genius. But when one is not a man of genius, and yet attempts to give counsel in times of difficulty, one should be above all things practical. Now, our relations with Ireland will not in any case be easily and soon made satisfactory; but while our middle class is what it is now, they never will. And our middle class, again, will not be easily and soon transformed; but while it gets its initiation to life through Salem House and Mr. Creakle, it never will.

The great thing is to initiate it to life by means of public schools. Public schools for the middle classes are not a panacea for our ills. No, but they are the indispensable preliminary to our real improvement on almost all the lines where as a nation we now move with embarrassment. If the consideration of our difficulties with Ireland had not, like so much else, brought me at last full upon this want,—which is capital, but far too little remarked,—I should probably not have ventured to intrude into the discussion of them. However terrified and dejected by the alarmists, I should have been inclined to bear my burden silently in that upper chamber in Grub Street, where I have borne in silence so many sorrows. I know that the professional people find the intervention of outsiders very trying in politics, and I have no wish to provoke their resentment. But when the discussion of any matter tends inevitably to show the crying need which there is for transforming our middle-class education, I cannot forbear from striking in; for if I do not speak of the need shown, nobody else will.

Yet the need is, certainly, great and urgent enough

to attract notice. But then our middle class is very strong and self-satisfied, and every one flatters it. It is like that strong and enormous creature described by Plato, surrounded by obsequious people seeking to understand what its noises mean, and to make in their turn the noises which may please it. At best, palliatives are now and then attempted; as there is a company, I believe, at this moment projected to provide better schools for the middle classes. Alas, I should not be astonished to find presently Mr. Creakle himself among the directors of a company to provide better schools for the middle classes, and the guiding spirit of its proceedings! so far, at least, as his magisterial functions, and his duties on philanthropical committees, and on committees of the Society of Arts, permit him to take part in them. But oftener our chief people take the bull by the horns, and actually congratulate the middle class on the character and conditions of its education. And so they play the part of a sort of spiritual pander to its defects and weaknesses, and do what in them lies to perpetuate them. Lord Frederick Cavendish goes down to Sheffield, to address an audience almost entirely trained by Salem House and by Mr. Creakle, and the most suitable thing he can find to say to them is, he thinks, to congratulate them on their energy and self-reliance in being so trained, and to give them to understand that he himself, if he were not Lord Frederick Cavendish, brought up at Cambridge, would gladly be Murdstone or Quinion, brought up by Mr. Creakle. But this is an old story, a familiar proceeding, for which the formula has long since been given : namely, that the upper class do not want to be disturbed in their preponderance, nor the middle class in their vulgarity. But if we wish cordially to attach Ireland to the English connexion, not only must we offer healing political measures, we must also, and that as speedily as we can, transform our middle class and its social civilisation.

I perceive that I have said little of faults on the side of the Irish, as I have said little of the merits which accompany, in our middle class, their failure in social civilisation. And for the same reason,—because the matter in hand was the failure on our part to do all in our power to attach Ireland, and how to set about remedying that failure. But as I have spoken with so much frankness of my own people and kindred, the Irish will allow me, perhaps, to end with quoting three queries of Bishop Berkeley's, and with recommending these to their attention :—

'1. Whether it be not the true interest of both nations to become one people, and whether either be sufficiently apprised of this ?

'2. Whether Ireland can propose to thrive so long as she entertains a wrong-headed distrust of England?

'3. Whether in every instance by which the Irish prejudice England, they do not in a greater degree prejudice themselves?'

Perhaps, our Irish friends might do well also to perpend the good bishop's caution against 'a general parturiency in Ireland with respect to politics and public counsel;' a parturiency which in clever young Irishmen does often, certainly, seem to be excessive. But, after all, my present business is not with the Irish but with the English;—to exhort my countrymen to healing measures and an attractive form of civilisation. And if one's countrymen insist upon it, that found to be sweet and attractive their form of civilisation is, or, if not, ought to be, then we who think differently must labour diligently to follow Burke's injunctions, and to 'dispose people to a better sense of their condition.'

AN UNREGARDED IRISH GRIEVANCE.

IN 1796, the very year before his death, when the political prospect for the people of Ireland seemed desperate, and all political struggle on their part useless and impotent, Burke wrote to an Irishman as follows :—

I should recommend to the middle ranks, in which I include not only all merchants, but all farmers and tradesmen, that they wouldchange as much as possible those expensive modes of living and that dissipation to which our countrymen in general are so much addicted. It does not at all become men in a state of persecution. They ought to conform themselves to the circumstances of a people whom Government is resolved not to consider as upon a par with their fellow-subjects. Favour they will have none. They must aim at other resources, and to make themselves independent *in fact* before they aim at a *nominal* independence. Depend upon it, that with half the privileges of the others, joined to a different system of manners, they would grow to a degree of importance to which, without it, no privileges could raise them, much less any intrigues or factious practices. I know very well that such a discipline, among so numerous a people, is not easily introduced, but I am sure it is not impossible. If I had youth and strength, I would go myself over to Ireland to work on that plan ; so certain I am that the well-being of all descriptions in the kingdom, as well as of themselves, depends upon a reformation amongst the Catholics. The work will be sure and slow in its operation, but it is certain in its effect. There is nothing which will not yield to perseverance and method.

Whether a sumptuary reform in the habits of the middle classes in Ireland is a crying need of the present hour, I have no sufficient means of judging. If it is, it is not a reform which we can well isolate from other needs, can well pursue by itself alone, and directly. It is a reform which must depend upon enlarging the minds and raising the aims of those classes ; upon humanising and civilising them. Expense in living, dissipation, are the first and nearest dangers, perhaps, to the Irish middle class, while its civilisation is low, because they are its first and nearest pleasures. They can only cease to be its first and nearest pleasures, if now they are so, by a rise in its standard of life, by an extending and deepening of its civilisation.

True, this greatly needs to be done. True, the improvement of Ireland, the self-government of Ireland, must come mainly through the middle class, and yet this class, defective in civilisation as it now is, is not ripe for the functions required of it. Its members have indeed to learn, as Burke says, 'to make themselves independent *in fact* before they aim at a *nominal* independence.' But not Ireland alone needs, alas, the lesson; we in England need it too. In England, too, power is passing away from the now governing class. The part to be taken in English life by the middle class is different from the part which the middle class has had to take hitherto,—different, more public, more important. Other and greater functions devolve upon this class than of old; but its defective civilisation makes it unfit to discharge them. It comes to the new time and to its new duties, it comes to them, as its flatterers will never tell it, but as it must nevertheless bear to be told and well to consider,—it comes to them with a defective type of religion, a narrow range of intellect and knowledge, a stunted sense of beauty, a low standard of manners.

The characters of defective civilisation in the Irish middle class are not precisely the same as in the English. But for the faults of the middle class in Ireland, as in England, the same remedy presents itself to start with; not a panacea by any means, not all-sufficient, not capable of working miracles of change in a moment, but yet a remedy sure to do good; the first and simplest and most natural remedy to apply, although it is left singularly out of sight, and thought, and mention. The middle class in both England and Ireland is the worst schooled middle class in Western Europe. Surely this may well have something to do with defects of civilisation! Surely it must make a difference to the civilisation of a middle class, whether it is brought up in ignoble schools where the instruction is nearly worthless, or in schools of high standing where the boy is carried through a well-chosen course of the best that has been known and said in the world! I, at any rate, have long been of opinion that the most beneficent reform possible in England, at present, is a reform about which hardly anybody seems to think or care,—the establishment of good public schools for the middle classes.

Most salutary for Ireland also would be the establishment of such schools there. In what state is the actual supply of schools for the middle classes in Ireland, we learn from a report lately published by a very acute observer, Professor Mahaffy, of Trinity College, Dublin. I propose to give here a short account of what he tells us, and to add a few thoughts which suggest themselves after reading him.

Professor Mahaffy was appointed by the Endowed Schools Commission in 1879 to visit and report upon the Grammar Schools of Ireland. He inspected the buildings and accommodations, attended the classes, examined the pupils; and he also visited some of the principal Grammar Schools in England, such as Winchester, Marlborough, Uppingham, and the City of London School, to provide himself with a definite standard of comparison. Professor Mahaffy is a man, as is well known, of brilliant attainments; he has had, also, great practical experience in teaching, and he writes with a freshness, plainness, and point which make his report very easy and agreeable reading.

The secondary schools of Ireland are classified by Professor Mahaffy as follows: the Royal Schools, the lesser schools managed by the Commissioners of Education, the Erasmus Smith's schools, the Incorporated Society's schools, the Protestant diocesan schools, the schools with private endowments, the Roman Catholic colleges, and the unendowed schools. He visited schools of each class. In all or almost all of them he found the instruction profoundly affected by the rules of the Intermediate Schools Commissioners. His report is full of remarks on the evil working of the examinations of this Intermediate Board, and he appears to consider the most important part of his business, as reporter, to be the delivering of his testimony against them. The Board arose, as is well known, out of the desire to do something for intermediate education in Ireland without encountering what is called the religious difficulty. 'The Liberal party has emphatically condemned religious endowment; the Protestants of Great Britain are emphatically hostile to the endowment of Catholicism in any shape or form.' We have all heard these parrot cries till one is sick of them. Schools, therefore, were not to be founded or directly aided, because this might be an endowment of Catholicism; but a system of examinations and prizes was established, whereby Catholic schools may be indeed aided indirectly, but so indirectly, it seems, as to suffer the consciences of the Protestants of Great Britain to remain at peace. Only this system of examinations and prizes, while good for the consciences of the Protestants of Great Britain, is very bad, in Professor Mahaffy's opinion, for the Irish schools. He insists on its evil effects in the very first page of his report, in speaking of the Royal School of Armagh, the chief of the Royal Schools, and the school with which he begins. He says :—

Under the rules of the Intermediate Commissioners it is found more advantageous to answer in a number of unimportant subjects, of which a hastily learned smattering suffices, than to study with earnestness the great subjects of education, —classics and mathematics. Hence, boys spend every leisure moment, and even part of their proper school-time, in learning little text-books on natural science, music, and even Irish, to the detriment of their solid progress. This is not all.

Owing to the appointing of fixed texts in classics and the paucity of new passages in the examination, the boys are merely crammed in the appointed texts without being taught real scholarship. When examining a senior division in classics, I observed that they all brought up annotated texts, in fact so fully annotated that every second clause was translated for them; and upon observing this to the master, he replied that he knew the evil, but that he could not get them through the intermediate course in any other way.

All through the report this is Professor Mahaffy's great and ever-recurring complaint: 'The multiplication of subjects supported by the Intermediate Board! which suit inaccurate and ill-taught pupils far better than those who learn the great subjects thoroughly.' Everywhere it struck him, that 'the boys, even when not over-worked, were addled with a quantity of subjects. They are taught a great many valuable truths; but they have not assimilated them, and only answer by accident. I have found this mental condition all over the country.' He calls the intermediate examinations 'the lowest and poorest of all public competitions.' The more intelligent of the schoolmasters, he says, condemn them:—

The principal (of the French college at Blackrock) has very large and independent views about education, which are well worthy of serious attention. He objects altogether to the intermediate examinations, and says that his profession is ruined by the complete subjugation of all school-work to the fixed programme, which is quite insufficient to occupy the better boys for a year, and which thus seriously impairs their progress. He also protests against the variety of unimportant subjects which produce fees for results, and thinks that a minimum of at least thirty-five per cent. should be struck off the answering, if these subjects are retained.

However, 'the false stimulus now supplied in the system of intermediate examinations established by Government' is too strong to be resisted :—

So strong a mercenary spirit has been excited both in masters and parents by this system, that all the schools in Ireland with one exception (the Friends' School in Waterford) have been forced into the competition; every boy is being taught the intermediate course, every error in the management of that course is affecting the whole country, and the best educator is unable to stem the tide, or do more than protest against any of the defects.

Professor Mahaffy is a hearty admirer of the great English public schools. He is of opinion, 'that what distinguishes the Englishman, all over the world, above men of equal breeding and fortune in other nations, is the training of those peculiar commonwealths, in which boys form a sort of constitution, and govern themselves under the direction of a higher authority.' But he thinks that the over-use of prize-competitions and examinations is doing harm in the great English schools too, though they are not yet enslaved by it as the Irish schools are:—

I find that by the spirit of the age, and the various requirements of many competitions, both English and Irish Schools have been driven into the great vice of multiplying subjects of instruction, and so crowding together hours of diverse teaching that the worst results must inevitably ensue. There is, in the first place, that enervating mental fatigue and consequent ill-health which is beginning to attract attention. When I visited Winchester it was easy to distinguish in a large class the boys who had won their way into the foundation by competition; they were remarkable for their worn and unhealthy looks. This evil, however, the evil of overwork at examination-courses, has already excited public attention, and is, I trust, in a fair way of being remedied. Nor did it strike me as at all so frequent, in Irish schools, as another mischief arising from the same cause. It rather appeared to me all over Ireland, and England also, that the majority of boys, without being over-worked, were *addled by the multiplicity* of their subjects, and instead of increasing their knowledge had utterly confused it. Whenever I asked the masters to point me out a brilliant boy, they replied that the race had died out. Is it conceivable that this arises from any inherent failing of the stock, and not rather from some great blundering in the system of our education? The great majority of thoughtful educators with whom I conferred agreed that it was due to this constant addition of new subjects;—to the cry after English grammar and English literature, and French and German, and natural science; to the subdivision of the wretched boys' time into two hours in the week for this, two hours for that, alternate days for this, alternate days for that ; in fact, to an injurious system of so teaching him everything that he can reason intelligently in nothing. I cannot speak too strongly of the melancholy impression forced upon me by the examination of many hundred boys in various schools through England and Ireland. I sought in vain for bright promise, for quick intelligence, for keen sympathy with their studies. It was not, I am sure, the boys' fault nor the masters'. It is the result of the present boa-constrictor system of competitive examination which is strangling our youth in its fatal embrace.

Professor Mahaffy finds fault with the Irish secondary schools as too often dirty and untidy, and ill-provided with proper accommodations. 'Whitewashing, painting, and scouring of floors are urgently needed ; indeed an additional supply of soap to the boys would not come amiss.' He notices the Jesuit College of St. Stanislaus, and a school at Portarlington, as signal exceptions. In general 'the floors are so filthy as to give a grimy and disgusting appearance to the whole room ; people are so accustomed to this in all Irish schools that they wonder at my remarking it.' At the chief of the Erasmus Smith's Schools, the high school in Dublin, 'I was detained,' he tells us, 'some time at the door, owing to the deafness of the porter, and thus having ample leisure to inspect the front of the house, found that the exceeding dirt of the windows made it pre-eminent, even among its shabbiest neighbours. I learned, on inquiry, that most of the window-sashes are not moveable. It is surprising that the members of the Board are not offended by this aspect of squalor and decay. I found the playground a mass of mud, which was carried on the boys' boots all through the stairs and school-rooms, thus making the inside of the house correspond with the outside.' Professor Mahaffy finds fault with the 'wretched system of management' which prevails in the Endowed Schools,—a system which prevents needful reforms, which perpetuates inefficient arrangements and perpetuates the employment of incompetent teachers, 'old and wearied men.' Those who elect the master, he says of the Clonmel School, 'are two absent lords; and I suppose a more unlikely Board to select a good schoolmaster could not easily be found. In the present case a rule has been followed the very opposite of that which prevails in England. There a schoolmaster retires upon a living; here a clergyman has retired from a living upon a school.' In another school, where the head-master is well qualified, Professor Mahaffy finds the assistant-master stopping the way :—

But when we come to the assistant-master we find things in a deplorable condition. He holds his place by appointment of the patron, and is not removable by the head-master or Commissioners, or perhaps by any one. The present usher is a man of about eighty or ninety years of age, indeed he may possibly be one hundred; he is so dull and shrivelled with age that he only comes in late and is unable to teach anything. I do not think he comprehended who I was or what I wanted. His appointment dates from the remote past, and when I asked what his qualifications were or had once been, I could learn nothing but some vague legends about his great severity in early youth; in fact, I was told *he had once pult the ear off a boy.* But these were venerable traditions.

Finally, Professor Mahaffy finds fault with that which is our signal deficiency in England also, the want of all general organisation of the service of secondary instruction, of all co-ordination of the existing resources scattered over the country :—

The general impression produced by a survey of the Irish Grammar Schools is this, that while there are many earnest and able men engaged in teaching and in improving the condition of education, all these efforts are individual efforts or scattered efforts, and the results produced are vastly inferior to those which might be expected from the existing national endowments both of money and of talent. For the Irish nation, with all its patent faults, is a clever nation; Irish boys are above the average in smartness and versatility. If the system of education were at all perfect, great intellectual results might fairly be expected.

Still, the tyranny of the intermediate course, and the bad effects it is producing on the Irish schools, are so completely the governing idea in our reporter's mind, that after enumerating all other hindrances to secondary instruction in Ireland, he cannot but return to this chief hindrance and conclude with it. He laments that the better endowed schools, at any rate, were not excluded by the Act from competing, and from ruining their school-course accordingly :—

For my own part, I feel constrained to recommend (to Irish parents for their sons) schools in England or elsewhere, where this enslaving system has not penetrated. It may no doubt act as a great stimulus to bad schools, and to a low type of scholars, who had otherwise been subject to no test whatever. To all higher schools, and to the higher class of boys who desire and deserve a real education in literature and science, this competition is an almost unmixed evil. To the real schoolmaster, who desires to develop the nature of his boys after his own fashion and by his own methods, such a system is a death-blow. The day will yet come, when men will look back on the mania in our legislation for competition as the anxious blundering of honest reformers, who tried to cure the occasional abuses of favouritism by substituting universal hardships, and to raise the tone of lower education by levelling down the higher, by substituting diversity for depth, and by destroying all that freedom and leisure in learning which are the true conditions of solid and lasting culture.

Professor Mahaffy admires, as I have said, the public schools in England, and envies us them greatly. 'The English public school,' he says, 'remains and will remain a kind of training place to which no nation in Europe, not to say the Irish, can show a parallel.' I agree with him in admiring our great public schools; still, the capital failure of Ireland, in regard to secondary instruction, is exhibited by us also. We have indeed good schools in England, expensive but good, for the boys of the aristocratic and landed class, and of the higher professional classes, and for the sons of wealthy merchants and manufacturers. But it is not difficult to provide good schools for people who can and will, in considerable numbers, pay highly for them. Irish parents who belong to the aristocratic and landed class, or to the higher professional classes, or to the class of wealthy merchants and manufacturers, can and do send their sons to our English public schools, and get them well trained and taught there. Professor Mahaffy approves of their doing so. 'It is not in the least surprising, that Irish parents who can afford it should choose this system for the education of their boys. No foolish talk about patriotism, no idle rant about absenteeism, can turn any conscientious parent from studying, above all, his children's welfare, and if he visits the great public schools of England he will certainly be impressed with their enormous superiority.'

I cannot myself see any disadvantage, or anything but advantage, to an Irish boy in being trained at one of the English public schools. If, therefore, the middle class in Ireland could as a whole afford to use these schools, I should not bemoan its condition, or busy myself about reforming the state of secondary instruction in Ireland. But it cannot. The bulk of the middle class in Ireland cannot, and the bulk of the middle class in England cannot either. The real weak point in the secondary instruction of both countries is the same. M. Gambetta is the son, I am told, of a tradesman at Cahors, and he was brought up in the *lycée* of Cahors; a school not so delightful and historic as Eton, certainly, but with a status as honourable as that of Eton, and with a teaching on the whole as good. In what kind of schools are the sons of tradesmen in England and Ireland brought up? They are brought up in the worst and most ignoble secondary schools in Western Europe. Ireland has nothing to envy us here. For the great bulk of our middle class, no less than for the great bulk of hers, the school-provision is miserably inadequate.

It can only become adequate by being treated as a public service, as a service for which the State, the nation in its collective and corporate character, is responsible. This proposition I have often advanced and sufficiently expounded. To me its truth seems self-evident, and the practice of other countries is present, besides, to speak for it. I am not going to enlarge upon this theme now. I want rather to point out how it comes to pass, that in England and Ireland the truth is not accepted and acted upon, and what difference there is, in this respect, between the case of England and that of Ireland.

In England, secondary instruction is not a public service, popular politicians and speakers at public meetings would tell us, because of the individual energy and self-reliance of the Englishman, and his dislike to State-interference. No doubt, there is in the Englishman a repugnance to being meddled with, a desire to be let alone. No doubt, he likes to act individually whenever he can, and not to have recourse to action of a collective and corporate character. To make even popular education a public service was very difficult. It is only a few years since one might hear State-aided elementary schools described, as schools with the *State-taint* upon them. However, the expediency and necessity of making popular education a public service grew to appear so manifest, that the repugnance was overcome. So far as our popular education is concerned, the reproach of *State-taint* has disappeared from people's mouths and minds.

Now, to make middle-class education a public service is only less expedient and necessary than to make popular education a public service. But, as to popular education, the light has dawned upon the community here in England; as to middle-class education, it has not. To talk of the *State-taint* in this case, is still popular; and a prominent member of the governing class, such as Lord Frederick Cavendish, will go and extol a middle-class audience, composed of people with a defective type of religion, a narrow range of intellect and knowledge, a stunted sense of beauty, a low standard of manners,—he will positively go and extol them for their energy and self-reliance in not adopting the means most naturally and directly fitted to lift them out of this imperfect state of civilisation, and will win their delighted applause by doing so.

This is a phenomenon of our social politics which receives its explanation, as I have often said, only when we consider that the upper class amongst us does not wish to be disturbed in its preponderance, or the middle class in its vulgarity. Not that Lord Frederick Cavendish does not speak in perfect good faith. He takes as a general rule the native English conviction that to act individually is a wholesome thing, and thinks that he cannot be wrong in applying it in any novel case that may arise. Still, at the bottom of the mind of our governing class is an instinct, on this matter of education, telling it that a really good and public education of the middle class is the surest means of removing, in the end, those inferiorities which at present make our middle class impossible as a governing class, and our upper class indispensable; —and this removal it is not every one in a governing class who can desire, though every one ought to desire it.

That the middle class should seek not to be disturbed in its vulgarity may seem more strange. But here, too, is at bottom the native English instinct for following one's individual course, for not being meddled with. Then, also, what most strongly moves and attaches, or has most strongly moved and attached hitherto, the strongest part of our middle class, the Puritan part, is the type of religion to which their nature and circumstances have since the Reformation led them. Now, to this type of religion, the State, or the nation acting as a whole in its collective and corporate character, has in general not been favourable. They are apprehensive, then, that to their religion a training in the schools of the State might not be favourable. Indeed, to the whole narrow system of life, arising out of the peculiar conjunction of the second great interest of their lives, business, with the first great interest of their lives, religion,—a system of life now become a second nature to them and greatly endeared to their hearts,—they are apprehensive that the wider ideas and larger habits of public schools might not be favourable. And so they are, on their part, as little forward to make middle-class education a public service, as the governing class, on their part, are little forward to do so. And although the necessities of the future, and a pressing sense of the defects of its actual civilisation, will in the end force the middle class to change its line and to demand what it now shrinks from, yet this has not happened yet, and perhaps may not happen for some years to come, may not happen in our life-time.

If, therefore, secondary instruction remains in a very faulty and incoherent state in England, at least it is by the English nation's own doing that it remains so. The governing class here is not seriously concerned to make it adequate and coherent; it is, on the contrary, indisposed to do so. That governing class will do what is actually desired and demanded of it by the middle class, by the class on whose favour political power depends; but it will do no more. The middle class, again, the class immediately concerned, has not yet acquired sufficient lucidity of mind to desire public schools, and to demand the resolute investigation and appliance of the best means for making them good. It has no such simple and logical aims governing its mind in this matter. A coherent system of public middle-class schools it does not at present want at all. Aims of quite another sort govern our middle class, whenever anything has to be done in regard to education. Its Protestant feelings must be respected, openings must be provided as far as possible for its children, and whatever is done must be plausible. And the governing class will always take good care to meet its wishes.

Professor Mahaffy will find that the things which so disturb his peace as a lover of education are all due to this cause : that the English middle class has aims quite other than the direct aim of making education efficient, and that the governing class, in whatever it does, respects and consults these aims of the middle class. He complains of the Intermediate Board and its system of prizes and examinations. But what would he have? Something had to be done for Irish secondary instruction. But the English public was by no means simply bent on doing what was best for this; alas, it is not even bent on doing what is best for its own! Something, I say, had to be done in Ireland for secondary instruction; but, in doing it, the Protestant feelings of the public of

Great Britain must before all things be respected. 'The Liberal party has emphatically condemned religious endowment ; the Protestants of Great Britain are implacably hostile to the endowment of Catholicism in any shape or form.' And the Government paid all due respect to these Liberal and Protestant feelings. Hence the Intermediate Board.

The whole system of perpetual competitive examinations everywhere, which Professor Mahaffy thinks so fatal, and which he attributes to the anxious blundering of honest reformers trying to cure the occasional abuses of favouritism, is he right in so attributing it ? Surely not ; there was no such blundering as he speaks of, because there was no desire to discover and do what was positively best in the matter. But the great British middle-class public had a desire to procure as many openings as possible for its children, and the Government could gratify this desire, and also relieve itself of responsibility. Hence our competitive examinations. The composition of the Boards and Commissions for Education, again, on which so much depends when studies have to be organised and programmes laid down, Professor Mahaffy is dissatisfied with them. He wants, he says, 'one responsible body, not made up altogether of lords and bishops and judges who give their spare moments to such duties, but mainly of practical educators. No one is so likely to be led away by novelties as the elderly amateur in education, who knows nothing of its practical working, and legislates on specious theories. So long as Boards in Ireland are chiefly made up of people of social or political importance only, education will not prosper.' But does Professor Mahaffy imagine that the British public has a fancy for a lucid and logical-minded Board, simply bent on perfecting education? Not at all! it wants a Board that is plausible; and the Government, whenever it institutes a Board, at least does its best to make a plausible one. Hence the 'lords and bishops and judges;' hence the 'elderly amateur.' Professor Mahaffy anticipates that the new Irish University will probably be arranged like the Intermediate Board, and not as a lover of education would desire. On that point I will give no opinion; all I am sure of is that it will be arranged plausibly. That is what our middle-class public want, and the Government will certainly accomplish it.

No, the great English middle-class public is at present by no means bent seriously on making education efficient all round. It prefers its routine and its claptrap to even its own education. It is and must be free to do so, if it likes. We who lament its doing so, we who see what it loses by doing so, we can only resolve not to be dupes of its claptrap ourselves, and not to help in duping others with it, but to work with patience and perseverance for the evocation of that better spirit which will surely arise in this great class at last.

Meanwhile, however, the English middle-class sacrifices to its routine and claptrap not only its own education, but the education of the Irish middle-class also. And this is certainly hard. It is hard, that is, if the Irish middle-class is not of one mind with it in the matter, does not share in its routine and claptrap, and prefer them to its own education. I suppose no one will dispute that the type of secondary instruction in the Intermediate Board, the type of superior instruction in the new Irish University, is determined by that maxim regnant, as we are told, in the middle-class electorate of Great Britain: 'The Liberal party has emphatically condemned religious endowment.' And this when we have, in Great Britain, Oxford and Cambridge, and Eton and Winchester, and the Scotch universities! And one of the organs of the British Philistine expresses astonishment at my thinking it worth while at the present day to collect Burke's Irish writings,—says that the state of things with which Burke had to deal is now utterly gone, that he had to deal with Protestant ascendency, and that 'the Catholics have now not a single cause of complaint.' As if the

Intermediate Board, as if the new Irish University, determined in the manner they are, and from the motives they are, were not in themselves evidences of the continued reign of Protestant ascendency!

But not only has Ireland a just claim not to have her education determined by the 'Protestant feelings' of Great Britain. She has a just claim not to have it determined by other feelings, also, of our British public, which go to determine it now. She has a just claim, in short, to have it determined as she herself likes. It is a plea, as I have elsewhere said, for Home Rule, if the way of dealing with education, and with other like things, which satisfies our Murdstones and Quinions, but does not satisfy people of quicker minds, is imposed on these people when they desire something better, because it is the way which our Murdstones and Quinions know and like. The Murdstones and Quinions of our middle class, with their strong individuality and their peculiar habits of life, do not want things instituted by the State, by the nation acting in its collective and corporate character. They do not want State schools, or State festivals, or State theatres. They prefer their Salem House, and their meeting, and their music-hall, and to be congratulated by Lord Frederick Cavendish upon their energy and self-reliance. And this is all very well for the Murdstones and Quinions, since they like to have it so. But it is hard that they should insist on the Irishman, too, acting as if he had the same peculiar taste, if he have not.

With other nations, the idea of the State, of the nation in its collective and corporate character, instituting means for developing and dignifying the national life, has great power. Such a disposition of mind is also more congenial, perhaps, to the Irish people likewise, than the disposition of mind of our middle class in Great Britain. The executive Government in Ireland is a very different thing from the executive Government in England, and has a much more stringent operation. But it does little, nevertheless, in this sense of giving effect to aspirations of the national life for developing and raising itself. Dublin Castle is rather a bureau of management for governing the country in compliance, as far as possible, with English ideas.

If the Irish desire to make the State do otherwise and better in Ireland than it does in England, if they wish their middle-class education, for instance, to be a public service with the organisation and guarantees of a public service, they may fairly claim to have these wishes listened to. And listened to, if they are clearly formed, rationally conceived, and steadily persisted in, such wishes ultimately must be. It would be too monstrous that Ireland should be refused an advantage which she desires, and which all our civilised neighbours on the Continent find indispensable, because the middle class in England does not care to claim for itself the advantage in question. The great thing is for the Irish to make up their own minds clearly on the matter. Do they earnestly desire to make their middle-class education adequate and efficient ; to leave it no longer dependent on 'individual efforts, scattered efforts ; ' to rescue it from its dirt and dilapidation, and from such functionaries as the aged assistant *who once pult the car off a boy*? Then let them make it a public service. Does Professor Mahaffy wish to relieve Irish boys from the unintelligent tyranny of endless examinations and competitions, and from being 'stupefied by a multiplicity of subjects' ? Let him, then, get his countrymen to demand that their secondary instruction shall be made a public service, with the honest, single-minded, logically pursued aim of efficiency.

Then these questions as to studies, competitions, and examinations will come,—as with us at present, whether in England or in Ireland, they never come,—under responsible review by a competent mind ; and this is what is wanted. The 'personages of high social standing,' the 'lords and bishops and judges,' the 'elderly amateur,' of whom Professor Mahaffy complains, will cease to potter; and we shall have, instead, the responsible review of a competent mind. Ireland will not only be doing good to herself by demanding this, by obtaining this; she will also be teaching England and the English middle class how to live.

ECCE, CONVERTIMUR AD GENTES.[1]

I CANNOT help asking myself how I come to be standing here to-night. It not unfrequently happens to me, indeed, to be invited to make addresses and to take part in public meetings,—above all in meetings where the matter of interest is education ; probably because I was sent, in former days, to acquaint myself with the schools and education of the Continent, and have published reports and books about them. But I make it a general rule to decline the invitation. I am a school-inspector under the Committee of Council on Education, and the Department which I serve would object, and very properly object, to have its inspectors starring it about the country, making speeches on education. An inspector must naturally be prone to speak of that education of which he has particular cognisance, the education which is administered by his own Department, and he might be supposed to let out the views and policy of his Depart-

[1] An Address delivered to the Ipswich Working Men's College.

ment. Whether the inspectors really knew and gave the Department's views or not, their speeches might equally be a cause of embarrassment to their official superiors.

However, I have no intention of compromising my official superiors by talking to you about that branch of education which they are concerned in administering,— elementary education. And if I express a desire that they should come to occupy themselves with other branches of education too, branches with which they have at present no concern, you may be quite sure that this is a private wish of my own, not at all prompted by my Department. You may rely upon it, that the very last thing desired by that Department itself, is to invade the provinces of education which are now independent of it. Nobody will ever be able to accuse the Committee of Council of carrying an Afghanistan war into those provinces, when it might have remained quietly within its own borders. There is a Latin law-maxim which tells us that it is the business of a good judge to seek to extend his jurisdiction :—*Boni judicis est ampliare jurisdictionem.* That may be characteristic of a good judge, but it is not characteristic of a British Government in domestic affairs generally, certainly not in the concerns of education.

And for this reason : because the British Government

is an aristocratic government. Such a government is entirely free from the faults of what is commonly called a bureaucracy. It is not meddlesome, not fussy, not prone to seek importance for itself by meddling with everybody and everything; it is by nature disposed to leave individuals and localities to settle their own affairs for themselves as much as possible. The action of individuals and of localities, left to themselves, proves insufficient in this point and in that; then the State is forced to intervene. But what I say is, that in all those domestic matters, such as the regulation of workhouses, or of factories, or of schools, where the State has, with us, been forced to intervene, it is not our aristocratic executive which has sought the right of intervention, it is public opinion which has imposed the duty of intervention upon our aristocratic executive. Our aristocratic system may have its faults, but the mania for State-interference everywhere is not one of them. Above all, in regard to education this has been conspicuously the case. Government did not move in the matter while it could avoid moving.

Of course, even when it was at last obliged to move, there were some people to be found who cried out against it for moving. In the early days of the Committee of Council, one clergyman wrote that he was not going to suffer Lord John Russell, 'or any other Turkish Bashaw,' to send an inspector into his schools ; and Archdeacon Denison threatened, as is well known, to have the poor inspector drowned in a horsepond. But these were eccentric men, living in a fantastic world of their own. To men who inhabit the real world, it was abundantly apparent that our Government moved in the matter of public education as late as it could, that it moved as slowly as it could, as inoffensively as it could ; and that throughout, instead of stimulating public opinion to give it additional powers, it has confined itself to cautiously accepting and discharging the functions which public opinion has insisted on laying upon it.

You may be sure that this will continue to be the case ; that if more part in public education comes to be assigned to the Government in this country, it is not that the Government seeks it, it is that the growth of opinion will compel the Government to undertake it. So that if I speak of the desirableness of extending to a further class of schools the action of the State, it is well understood that I am not, as in bureaucratic Prussia I might be, revealing the secret aims and ambitions of the Education Department. All the aims of that Department have been clearly manifested to be the other way.

Well, but why am I here ? I am here, in the first

place, because I heard that your Working Men's College, which holds its annual meeting to-night, and which I was asked to address, is the largest body of the kind in England. Bodies of this kind, with their classes, their lectures, their libraries, their aspirations, are a testimony, however poor and imperfect may be the use often made of them, they are, as it seems to me, a testimony, they are a profession of faith, which is both affecting and valuable. They are a profession of belief in the saving power of light and intelligence, a profession of belief in the use and in the practicability of trying to know *oneself* and the world, *to follow*, as Dante says, *virtue and knowledge*.

No one can accuse us English, as a nation, of being too forward with such professions of faith in the things of the mind. No one can accuse us of not showing ourselves enough aware, how little good may in many cases come from professions of this sort, how much they may disappoint us, what a contrast their performance often is to their promise, how much they often bring with them which is hollow and nonsensical. We are very shy, as every one knows, of all public homage to the power of science and letters. We have no National Institute. In a short time there will be held in Paris a reception, as it is called, of one of the most famous men of letters in France, or indeed in all Europe,—M. Renan,—at the French

Academy. That reception, and the discourse of the new member, will be for our neighbours over in France one of the very foremost events of the year. Hardly any parliamentary field-day will call forth greater interest and excitement. Every one will want to be present, every one will be eager to know what is said, every one will discuss what is said. We English keenly feel the unreality, as we call it, which attends displays of this kind. We prefer that our own celebrations should be for incidents of a more practical character; should be such as the dinner and speechifying, for instance, at the opening of the annual season for the Buckhounds.

But above all, we are on our guard against expecting too much from institutions like this Working Men's College. We are reminded what grand expectations Lord Brougham and the other friends of knowledge cheap and popular, the founders of the Mechanics' Institutes, held out; what tall talk they indulged in; and we are told to look and see how little has come of it all. Nature herself fights against them and their designs, we are told. At the end of his day, tired with his labour, the working man in general cannot well have the power, even if he have the will, to make any very serious and fruitful efforts in the pursuit of knowledge. Whatever high professions these institutions may start with, inevitably their members will come, it is said, to decline upon a lower range of claim and endeavour. They will come to content themselves with seeking mere amusement and relaxation from their Institute. They will visit its reading-rooms merely to read the newspapers, to read novels; and they are not to be blamed for it.

No, perhaps they are not to be blamed for it, even if this does happen. And yet the original, lofty aspiration, the aspiration after the satisfactions, solace, and power which are only to be got from true knowledge, may have been right after all. In spite of the frequent disappointment, the constant difficulty, it may have been right. For to arrive at a full and right conception of things, to know one's self and the world,—which is knowledge; then to act firmly and manfully on that knowledge,—which is virtue; this is the native, the indestructible impulse of the spirit of man. All the high-flown commonplaces about the power of knowledge, and about the mind's instinctive desire of it, have their great use, whenever we can so put them as to feel them animating and inspiring to us. For they are true in themselves; only they are discredited by being so often used insincerely. The profession of faith of institutes like your College, that knowledge is power, that there is an intelligible law of things, that the human mind seeks to arrive at it, and that our welfare depends on our arriving at it and obeying it, this profession of faith, I say, is sound in itself, it is precious, and we do well to insist upon it. It puts in due prominence a quality which does not always get enough regard in this country,—intelligence.

Goethe, the great poet of Germany, and the greatest critic, perhaps, that has ever lived, went so far as to say boldly of our nation (which, notwithstanding, he highly esteemed and admired) : *Der Engländer ist eigentlich ohne Intelligenz*—' The Englishman is, properly speaking, without intelligence.' Goethe by no means meant to say that the Englishman was stupid. All he meant was, that the Englishman is singularly without a keen sense of there being an intelligible law of things, and of its being our urgent business to ascertain it and to make our doings conform to it. He meant that the Englishman is particularly apt to take as the rule of things what is customary, or what falls in with his prepossessions and prejudices, and to act upon this stoutly and without any misgiving, as if it were the real natural rule of things. He meant that the Englishman does not much like to be told that there is a real natural rule of things, presenting itself to the intelligence; to be told that our action, however energetic, is not safe unless it complies with this real and intelligible rule. And I think Goethe was right here, and that the Englishman, from his insularity, and from his strength, and from some want of suppleness in his mind, does often answer to the description which Goethe gives of him.

Now it is a grave thing, this indifference to the real natural and rational rule of things, because it renders us very liable to be found fighting against nature, and that is always calamitous. And so I come at last to the entire reason for my being here to-night. There is a point, in which our action, as a community, seems to me quite at variance with what the rational rule of things would prescribe, and where we all suffer by its being thus at variance. I have tried in vain for twenty years to make the parties most directly concerned see the mischief of the present state of things. I want to interest you in the matter. I speak to you as a Working Men's College, the largest in England, representing the profession of faith that what we need is intelligence, the power to see things as they really are, and to shape our action accordingly. I look upon you, I say, as representing that profession of faith, and representing it as entertained by the class of working men. You, too, are concerned in the failure which I want to remedy, though not directly concerned in it. But you *are* concerned in it, and that gravely; we are all gravely concerned in it.

You will, I am sure, suffer me to speak to you with perfect frankness, even though what I say should offend some of those who hear me. My address is to the class of working men; but there are present before me to-night, I know, hearers from other classes too. However, the only possible use of my coming here would be lost if I did not speak to you with perfect frankness. I am no politician. I have no designs upon your borough, or upon any borough, or upon parliamentary honours at all. Indeed, I have no very ardent interest,—if you will allow me to speak for a moment of myself and of what interests me,—in politics in their present state in this country. What interests me is English civilisation; and our politics in their present state do not seem to me to have much bearing upon that.

English civilisation,—the humanising, the bringing into one harmonious and truly humane life, of the whole body of English society,—that is what interests me. I try to be a disinterested observer of all which really helps and hinders that. Certain hindrances seem to me to be present with us, and certain helps to be wanting to us. An isolated observer may easily be mistaken, and his observations greatly require the test which other minds can exert upon them. If I fail to carry you with me in what seems to me to be perfectly clear, that is against the soundness of my observations and conclusions. But that I may have the chance of carrying you with me, it is necessary that I should speak to you with entire frankness. Then it will appear whether your aid, or the aid of any among you, is to be had for removing what seems to me one great hindrance, and for providing what seems to me one great help, to our civilisation.

For twenty years, then,—ever since I had to go about the Continent to learn what the schools were like there, and observed at the same time the people for whom the schools existed and the conditions of their life, and compared it with what was to be found at home,—ever since that time, I have felt convinced that for the progress of our civilisation, here in England, three things were above all necessary :—a reduction of those immense inequalities of condition and property amongst us, of which our land-system is the base; a genuine municipal system; and public schools for the middle classes. I do not add popular education. Even so long as twenty years ago, popular education was already launched. I was myself continually a witness of the progress it was making; I could see that the cause of popular education was safe. The three points, then, were reduction of our immense inequalities of condition and property, a municipal system extended all through the country, and public schools for the middle classes. These points are hardly dreamed of in our present politics, any one of them.

Take the first of the three. Mr. Gladstone, who ought to know, ridicules the very notion of a cry for equality in this country; he says that the idea of equality has never had the slightest influence upon English politics; nay, that, on the contrary, we have the religion of inequality. There is, indeed, a little bill brought forward in Parliament year after year,—the Real Estates Intestacy Bill,—which proposes that there should be equality in the division of a man's land amongst his children after his death, in case he happens to die without a will. It is answered, that if a man wants his land to go thus equally amongst his children, he has only just to take the trouble of making a will to that effect; and that, in the absence of a will, his land had better follow the rule of the present general system of landed inheritance in this country, a system which works well. And nothing more is said, except, perhaps, that one hears a few timid words of complaint about the hardship inflicted upon younger children by this system.

But, for my part, I am not so much concerned about the younger children. My objection to the present system is not on their account; but because I think that, putting their supposed natural rights quite out of the question, the present system does not work well now at all, but works altogether badly. I think that now, however it may have worked formerly, the system tends to materialise our upper class, vulgarise our middle class, brutalise our lower class. If it does not do that, I have no other objection to make to it. I do not believe in *any* natural rights; I do not believe in a natural right, in each of a man's children, to his or her equal share of the father's property. I have no objection to the eldest son taking all the land, or the youngest son, or the middle daughter, on one condition : that this state of things shall really work well, that it shall be for the public advantage.

Once our present system of landed inheritance had its real reason and justification,—it worked well. When the modern nations of Europe were slowly building themselves up out of the chaos left by the dissolution of the Roman empire, a number of local centres were needed for the process, with a strong hereditary head-man over each; and this natural need the feudal land-system met. It seems to me, it has long seemed to me, that, the circumstances being now quite changed, our system of immense inequalities of condition and property works not well but badly, has the natural reason of things not for it but against it. It seems to me that the natural function is gone, for which an aristocratic class with great landed estates was required ; and that when the function is gone, and the great estates with an infinitely multiplied power of ministering to mere pleasure and indulgence remain, the class owning them inevitably comes to be materialised, and the more so the more the development of industry and ingenuity augments the means of luxury.

The action of such a class materialises all the class of newly enriched people as they rise. The middle class, having above them this materialised upper class, with a wealth and luxury utterly out of their reach, with a standard of social life and manners, the offspring of that wealth and luxury, seeming utterly out of their reach also, are inevitably thrown back too much upon themselves, and upon a defective type of civilisation. The lower class, with the upper class and its standard of life still further out of their reach, and finding nothing to attract them or to elevate them in the standard of life of the middle classes, are inevitably, in their turn, thrown back upon themselves, and upon a defective type of civilisation. I speak of classes. In all classes, there are individuals with a happy nature and an instinct for the humanities of life, who stand out from their class, and who form exceptions.

Now, the word *vulgarised* as applied to the middle class, and *brutalised* as applied to the lower class, may seem to you very hard words. And yet some of you, at any rate, will feel that there is a foundation for them. And whether you feel it or not, the most competent, the most dispassionate observers feel it, and use words about it much more contemptuous and harsher than mine. The question is not, whether you or I may feel the truth of a thing of this kind; the question is, whether the thing is really so. I believe that it is so; that with splendid qualities in this nation at large, that with admirable exceptions to be found in all classes, we at present do tend to have our higher class in general materialised, our middle class vulgarised, and our lower class brutalised; and that this tendency we owe to what Mr. Gladstone calls our religion of inequality.

True, no one here in England combines the fact of the defects in our civilisation with the fact of our enormous inequality. People may admit the facts separately; the inequality, indeed, they cannot well deny; but they are not accustomed to combine them. But I saw, when I began to think about these matters, that elsewhere the best judges combined this fact of great social imperfection with the fact of great inequality. I saw that Turgot, the best and wisest statesman whom France has ever had, himself one of the governing and fortunate class, made inequality answerable for much of the misery of the modern nations of Europe. 'Everywhere,' says Turgot, 'the laws have favoured that inequality of fortunes which corrupts a certain number, to doom the rest to degradation and misery.' Vehement as this language sounds, I saw that the spectacle France is described as presenting, under the old system, was enough to account for it. I saw that the French peasants, under that system, were described by a sober and grave authority as presenting the appearance of a number of puny, dingy, miserable creatures, half clad and half articulate, creeping about on the surface of the ground and feebly scratching it. I saw that Tocqueville, coming after the French Revolution, and a severe judge of its faults and of the faults of democracy, spoke of inequality much as Turgot spoke of it. 'The common people is more uncivilised in aristocratic countries,' says Tocqueville, ' than in any others, because there, where persons so powerful and so rich are met with, the weak and the poor feel themselves overwhelmed, as it were, with the weight of their own inferiority; not finding any point by which they may recover equality, they despair of themselves altogether, and suffer themselves to fall into degradation.'

And then I saw the French peasant of the present day, who has been made by equality. There is a chorus of voices from all sides in praise of his condition. First let us take, as in duty bound, your principal, Mr. Barham Zincke, who has been staying in a French peasant's home this last summer, and has published in the *Fortnightly Review*, in two delightful articles which ought to be reprinted in a cheap form, an account of what he beheld.[1] Your principal says that 'the dense peasant population of the Limagne,'—the region where he was staying, in the heart of France,—'are, speaking of them as a body, honest, contented, hard-working, hardy, self-respecting, thrifty, and self-supporting.' He gives a charming account of their manners and courtesy, as well as of their prosperity; and he pronounces such a population to be a State's greatest wealth. Prince Bismarck appears to agree with your principal, for he declares that the social condition of France seems to have greater elements of soundness, —this well-being of the French peasant counting foremost among them all,—than the social condition of any other nation of Europe. A learned Belgian economist, M. de Laveleye, chimes in with Prince Bismarck and with your principal, and declares that France, being the country of Europe where the soil is more divided than anywhere else except in Switzerland and Norway, is, at the same time, the country where material well-being is most widely spread, where wealth has of late years increased most,

[1] See *Fortnightly Review* for November and December, 1878.

and where population is least outrunning those limits which, for the comfort and progress of the working classes themselves, seem necessary. Finally, I come back again to another countryman of our own, Mr. Hamerton, who lives in France. He speaks of the French peasant just as your principal speaks of him, and he ends by saying : 'The interval between him and a Kentish labourer is enormous.' What, that black little half-human creature of the times before the Revolution, feebly scratching the earth's surface, and sunk far below the point which any English peasantry ever sank to, has now risen to this, that the interval between him and a Kentish labourer,—no such bad specimen of our labourers either,—is enormous ! And this has been brought about by equality.

Therefore, both the natural reason of the thing and also the proof from practical experience seem to me to show the same thing : that for modern civilisation some approach to equality is necessary, and that an enormous inequality like ours is a hindrance to our civilisation. This to me appears so certain, that twenty years since, in a preface to a book about schools, I said that I thought so. I said the same thing more at length quite lately, in a lecture [1] at the Royal Institution, an institution which

---

[1] Published in the *Fortnightly Review* for March, 1878 ; and reprinted in *Mixed Essays*, with the title *Equality*.

has been stigmatised by a working man as being 'the most aristocratic place in England.' I repeat it here because it is a thing to be thought over and examined in all its bearings, not pushed away out of sight. If our inequality is really unfavourable to our civilisation, sooner or later this will be perceived generally, and our inequality will be abated. It will be abated by some measure far beyond the scope of our present politics, whether by the adoption of the French law of bequest, which now prevails so widely upon the Continent, or, as Mr. Mill thought preferable, by fixing the maximum of property which any one individual may take by bequest or inheritance, or in some other manner. But this is not likely to come in our time, nor is it to be desired that such a change should come while we are yet ill prepared for it. It is a matter to which I greatly wish to direct your thoughts, and to direct the thoughts of all who think seriously. I enlarge upon it to-night, because it renders so very necessary a reform in another line, to which I shall come finally. But it is not itself a matter where I want to enlist your help for a positive present measure of reform.

Neither is the matter which I am next going to mention a matter of this kind. My second point, you remember, was the extension of municipal organisation throughout the whole country. No one in England seems to imagine that municipal government is applicable except in towns. All the country districts are supposed to require nothing more than the parish vestry, answering to that sort of mass-meeting of the parishioners in the churchyard, under the presidency of the parson, after service on Sundays, which Turgot describes in the country districts of France before the Revolution. Nothing, as I have frequently said, struck me more, both in France and elsewhere on the Continent, than the working of the municipality and municipal council as established everywhere, and to observe how it was the basis of all local affairs, and the right basis. For elementary schools, for instance, the municipal basis is undoubtedly the natural and right one; and we are embarrassed, and must be embarrassed, so long as we have not the municipal basis to use for them in the rural districts of this country. For the peasant, moreover, for the agricultural labourer, municipal life is a first and invaluable stage in political education; more helpful by far, because so much more constant, than the exercise of the parliamentary franchise. So this is my second point to which I should like members of institutions like yours to turn their thoughts, as a thing very conducive to that general civilisation which it is the object of all cultivating of our intelligence to bring about. But this, too,—the establishment of a genuine municipal system for the whole country,—will hardly, perhaps, come in our time; men's minds have not yet been sufficiently turned to it for that. I am content to leave this also as a matter for thought with you.

Not so with my third point, where I hope we may actually get something done in our time. I am sure, at all events, we *need* to get something actually done towards it in our time. I want to enlist your interest and help towards this object,—towards the actual establishment of public schools for the middle classes.

The topics which suggest themselves to me in recommendation of this object are so numerous that I hardly know which of them to begin with; and yet I have occupied your attention a good while already, and I must before long come to an end of my discourse. As I am speaking to a Working Men's College, I will begin with what is supposed to have most weight with people; I will begin with the direct interests in this matter of yourselves and your class. By the establishment of public schools for the middle classes I mean an establishment of the same kind as we now have for popular education. I mean the provision by law, throughout the country, of a supply of properly guaranteed schools, in due proportion to the estimated number of the population requiring them; schools giving secondary instruction, as it is called,—that fuller and higher instruction which comes after elementary instruction,—and giving it at a cost not exceeding a certain rate.

Now for your direct interest in the matter. You have a direct interest in having facilities to rise given to what M. Gambetta, that famous popular leader in France, calls the new social strata. This rise is chiefly to be effected by education. Promising subjects come to the front in their own class, and they pass then, by a second and higher stage of education, into the class above them, to the great advantage of society. It is hardly too much to say that you and your class have in England no schools by which you can accomplish this rise if you are worthy of it.

In France they exist everywhere. Your principal tells us, that he found in the village where he was staying in the Limagne, six village lads, peasants' children, who were attending the secondary schools in Clermont. After all their losses, after all the milliards they have had to pay to Germany, the French have been laying out more and more in the last few years on their public secondary schools; and they do not seem so much worse off in their pecuniary condition, at this moment, than practical nations which make no such expenditure. At this very time a commission is sitting in France, to consider whether secondary instruction may not be brought into closer connexion with elementary instruction than it is at present, by establishing schools more perfectly fitted than the present secondary schools to meet the wants of the best subjects who rise from the schools below.

Now, you often see the School Boards, here in this country, doing what is in my opinion an unwise thing, making the programme of their elementary schools too ambitious. The programme of the elementary school should be strictly limited. Those who are capable and desirous of going higher should do it either by means of evening classes such as you have here, or by means of secondary schools. But why do the School Boards make this mistake?—for a mistake I think it is, and it gives occasion to the enemies of popular education to represent it as an unpractical and pretentious thing. But why do they make the mistake? They make it because, in the total absence in this country of public secondary schools, and in the inconvenience arising from this state of things, they are driven to make some attempt to supply the deficiency. Discourage, then, the School Boards in their attempt to make the elementary school what it cannot well be; but make them join with you in calling for public secondary schools, which will accomplish properly what they are aiming at.

But all this is socialism, we are told. An excellent man, Professor Fawcett, tells us that the most marked characteristic of modern socialism is belief in the State. He tells us that socialism and recourse to the action of the State go always together. The argument is an unfortunate one just at this moment, when the most judicious of French newspapers, the *Journal des Débats*, informs us that in France, which we all consider a hotbed of State-action and of centralisation, socialism has quite disappeared. However, this may perhaps turn out not to be true. At any rate, Professor Fawcett says that the working men of this country cannot be too much cautioned against resort to the State, centralisation, bureaucracy, and the loss of individual liberty; that the working class cannot be too much exhorted to self-reliance and self-help.

Well, I should have thought that there had been no lack of cautions and exhortations in this sense to us English, whether we are working men or whatever we may be. Why, we have heard nothing else ever since I can remember! And ever since I was capable of reflexion I have thought that such cautions and exhortations might be wanted elsewhere, but that giving them perpetually in

England was indeed carrying coals to Newcastle. The inutility, the profound inutility, of too many of our Liberal politicians, comes from their habit of for ever repeating, like parrots, phrases of this kind. In some countries the action of the State is insufficient, in others it is excessive. In France it is excessive. But hear a real Liberal leader, M. Gambetta, in reply to the invectives of *doctrinaires* against the State and its action. 'I am not for the abuses of centralisation,' said M. Gambetta at Romans, 'but these attacks on *the State*, which is France, often make me impatient. I am a defender of *the State*. I will not use the word centralisation; but I am a defender of the national *centrality*, which has made the French nation what it now is, and which is essential to our progress.' Englishmen are not likely, you may be sure, to let the State encroach too much; they are not likely to be not lovers enough of individual liberty and of individual self-assertion. Our dangers are all the other way. Our dangers are in exaggerating the blessings of self-will and self-assertion, in not being ready enough to sink our imperfectly informed self-will in view of a large general result.

Do not suffer yourselves, then, to be misled by declamations against the State, against bureaucracy, centralisation, socialism, and all the rest of it. The State is just what Burke very well called it, long before M. Gambetta : *the nation in its collective and corporate character.* To use the State is simply to use co-operation of a superior kind. All you have to ask yourselves is whether the object for which it is proposed to use this co-operation is a rational and useful one, and one likely to be best reached in this manner. Professor Fawcett says that socialism's first lesson is, that the working man can acquire capital without saving, through having capital supplied to him by the State, which is to serve as a fountain of wealth perennially flowing without human effort. Well, to desire to use the State for that object is irrational, vain, and mischievous. Why? Because the object itself is irrational and impossible. But to use the State in order to get, through that high form of co-operation, better schools and better guaranteed schools than you could get without it, is rational, because the object is rational. The schools may be self-supporting if you like. The point is, whether by their being public schools, State schools, they are or are not likely to be better schools, and better guaranteed, than you could get in any other way. Indisputably they are likely to be better, and to give better guarantees. Well, then, this use of the State is a use of co-operation of a very powerful kind for a good and practicable purpose; and co-operation in itself is peculiarly of advantage, as I need not tell you, to the middling and ill off. Rely upon it that we English can use the State without danger; and that for you to be deceived by the cry against State-interference is to play the game of your adversaries, and to prolong for yourselves a condition of certain inferiority.

But I will ask you to do more than to consider your own direct interest in the establishment of public schools for the middle classes. I will ask you to consider the general interest of the community. The friends and flatterers of the middle-classes,—and they have many friends and flatterers,—have been in the habit of assuring us, that the predominance of the middle classes was all that we required for our well-doing. Mr. Bright, a man of genius, and who has been a great power in this country, has always seemed to think that to insure the rule of the middle clssses in this country would be to bring about the millennium. Perhaps the working class has not been without its flatterers too, who have assured it that it ought to rule becuase it was so admirable. But you will observe, that my great objection to our enormous inequality, and to our aristocratic system, is not that it keeps out from power worthier claimants of it, but that it so grievously mars and stunts both our middle class and our lower class, so keeps them in imperfection. It is not the faults and imperfections of our present ruling class itself which strike me so much. Its members have plenty of faults and imperfections, but as a whole they are the best, the most energetic, the most capable, the honestest upper class which the world has ever seen. What strikes me is the bad effect of their rule upon others.

The middle classes cannot assume rule as they are at present,—it is impossible. And yet in the rule of this immense class, this class with so many correspondences, communications, and openings into the lower class, lies our future. There I agree with Mr. Bright. But our middle class, as it is at present, *cannot* take the lead which belongs to it. It has not the qualifications. Seriousness it has, the better part of it; it may even be said to have sacrificed everything to seriousness. And of the seriousness and of the sense for conduct in this nation, which are an invaluable treasure to it, and a treasure most dangerously wanting elsewhere, the middle classes are the stronghold. But they have lived in a narrow world of their own, without openness and flexibility of mind, without any notion of the variety of powers and possibilities in human life. They know neither man nor the world; and on all the arduous questions presenting themselves to our age,—political questions, social questions, the labour question, the religious question,—they have at present no light, and can give none. I say, then, they *cannot* fill their right place as they are now; but you, and I, and every man in this country, are interested in their being able to fill it.

How are they to be made able? Well, schools are something. Schools are not everything; and even public schools, when you get them, may be far from perfect. Our public elementary schools are far from perfect. But they throw into circulation year by year among the working classes,—and here is the great merit of Mr. Forster's Act,—a number of young minds trained and intelligent, such as you never got previously; and this must tell in the long run. Our public secondary schools, when we get them, may be far from perfect. But they will throw into circulation year by year, among the middle classes, a number of young people with minds instructed and enlarged as they never are now, when their schools are, both socially and intellectually, the most inadequate that fall to the lot of any middle class among the civilised nations of Europe. And the improvement so wrought must tell in the end, and will gradually fit the middle classes to understand better themselves and the world, and to take their proper place, and to grasp and treat real politics,—politics far other than their politics of

Dissent, which seem to me quite played out. This will be a work of time. Do not suppose that a great change of this kind is to be effected off hand. But we may make a beginning for it at once, and a good beginning, by public schools for the middle classes.

For twenty years I have been vainly urging this upon the middle classes themselves. Now I urge it upon you. Comprehend, that middle-class education is a great democratic reform, of the truest, surest, safest kind. Christianity itself was such a reform. The kingdom of God, the grand object of Jesus Christ, the grand object of Christianity, is mankind raised, as a whole, into harmony with the true and abiding law of man's being, living as we were meant to live. Those of old who had to forward this work found the Jewish community,—to whom they went first,—narrow, rigid, sectarian, unintelligent, of impracticable temper, their heads full of some impossible politics of their own. Then they looked around, and they saw an immense world outside the Jewish community, a world with a thousand faults, no doubt, but with openness and flexibility of mind, new and elastic, full of possibilities;—and they said: *We turn to the Gentiles!* Do not be affronted at being compared to the Gentiles; the Gentiles were the human race, the Gentiles were the future. Mankind are called in one body to the peace of

God; that is the Christian phrase for civilisation. We have by no means reached that consummation yet ; but that, for eighteen centuries, we have been making way towards it, we owe to the Gentiles and to those who turned to them. The work, I say, is not nearly done yet ; and our Judaic and unelastic middle class in this country is of no present service, it seems, for carrying it forward. Do you, then, carry it forward yourselves, and insist on taking the middle class with you. You will be amply repaid for the effort, in your own fuller powers of life and joy, in any event. We may get in our time none of the great reforms which we have been talking about ; we may not even get public schools for the middle classes. But we are always the better, all of us, for having aimed high, for having striven to see and know things as they really are, for having set ourselves to walk in the light of that knowledge, to help forward great designs, and to do good. ' Consider whereunto ye are born ! ye were not made to live like brutes, but to follow virtue and knowledge.'

THE FUTURE OF LIBERALISM.

A PUBLIC man, whose word was once of great power and is now too much forgotten by us, William Cobbett, had a humorous way of expressing his contempt for the two great political parties that between them govern our country, the Whigs and Tories, or Liberals and Conservatives, and who, as we all know, are fond of invoking their principles. Cobbett used to call these principles, contemptuously, *the principles of Pratt, the principles of Yorke.* Instead of taking, in the orthodox style, the divinised heroes of each party, and saying *the principles of Mr. Pitt, the principles of Mr. Fox,* he took a Whig and a Tory Chancellor, Lord Camden and Lord Hardwicke, who were more of lawyers than of politicians, and upon them he fathered the principles of the two great parties in the State. It is as if a man were now to talk of Liberals and Conservatives adhering, not to *the principles of Mr. Gladstone, the principles of Lord Beaconsfield,* but to *the principles of Roundell Palmer, the principles of*

Cairns. Eminent as are these personages, the effect of the profession of faith would be somewhat attenuated ; and this is just what Cobbett intended. He meant to throw scorn on both of the rival parties in the State, and on their profession of principles ; and so this great master of effect took a couple of lawyers, whose names lent themselves happily to his purpose, and called the principles contending for mastery in Parliament, *the principles of Pratt, the principles of Yorke!*

Cobbett's politics were at bottom always governed by one master-thought,—the thought of the evil condition of the English labourer. He saw the two great parties in the State inattentive, as he thought, to that evil condition of the labourer,—inattentive to it, or ignorantly aggravating it by mismanagement. Hence his contempt for Whigs and Tories alike. And perhaps I may be allowed to compare myself with Cobbett so far as this : that whereas his politics were governed by a master-thought, the thought of the bad condition of the English labourer, so mine, too, are governed by a master-thought, but by a different one from Cobbett's. The master-thought by which my politics are governed is rather this, —the thought of the bad civilisation of the English middle class. But to this object of my concern I see the two great parties in the State as inattentive as, in Cobbett's regard, they were to the object of his. I see them inattentive to it, or ignorantly aggravating its ill state by mismanagement. And if one were of Cobbett's temper, one might be induced, perhaps, under the circumstances, to speak of our two great political parties as scornfully as he did ; and instead of speaking with reverence of the body of Liberal principles which recommend themselves by Mr. Gladstone's name, or of the body of Conservative principles which recommend themselves by Lord Beaconsfield's, to call them gruffly *the principles of Pratt, the principles of Yorke.*

Cobbett's talent any one might well desire to have, but Cobbett's temper is far indeed from being a temper of mildness and sweet reason, and must be eschewed by whoever makes it his study ' to liberate,' as Plato bids us, ' the gentler element in himself.' And therefore I will most willingly consent to call the principles of the Liberal and Conservative parties by their regular and handsome title of *the principles of Mr. Gladstone, the principles of Lord Beaconsfield,* instead of disparagingly styling them *the principles of Pratt, the principles of Yorke.* Only, while conceding with all imaginable willingness to Liberals and Conservatives the use of the handsomest title for their principles, (I have never been able to see that these principles of theirs, at any rate as they succeed in exhibiting them, have quite the value or solidity which their professors themselves suppose.

It is but the other day that I was remarking to confident Conservatives, at the very most prosperous hour of Conservative rule, how, underneath all external appearances, the country was yet profoundly Liberal. And eight or ten years ago, long before their disaster of 1874 came, I kept assuring confident Liberals that the mind of the country was grown a little weary of their stock performances upon the political stage, and exhorting my young Liberal friends not to be for rushing impetuously upon this stage, but to keep aloof from it for a while, to cultivate a disinterested play of mind upon the stock notions and habits of their party, and to endeavour to promote, with me, an inward working. Without attending to me in the least, they pushed on towards the arena of politics, not at that time very successfully. But they have, I own, been much more fortunate since; and now they stand in the arena of politics, not quite so young as in those days when I last exhorted them, but full of vigour still, and in good numbers. Me they have left staying outside as of old; unconvinced, even yet, of the wisdom of their choice, a Liberal of the future rather than a Liberal of the present, disposed to think that by its actual present words and works the Liberal party, however prosperous it may seem, cannot really succeed, that its practice wan's more of simple and sincere thought to direct it, and that our young friends are not taking the surest way to amend this state of things when they cast in their lot with it, but rather are likely to be carried away by the stream themselves.

However, politicians we all of us here in England are and must be, and I too cannot help being a politician; but a politician of that commonwealth of which the pattern, as the philosopher says, exists perhaps somewhere in heaven, but certainly is at present found nowhere on earth,—a Liberal, as I have said, of the future. Still, from time to time Liberals of the future cannot but be stirred up to look and see how their politics relate themselves to the Liberalism which now is, and to test by them the semblances and promises and endeavours of this,—especially at its moments of resurrection and culmination,—and to forecast what its fortunes are likely to be. And this one does for one's own sake first and foremost, and for the sake of the very few who may happen to be likeminded with oneself, to satisfy a natural and irresistible bent for seeing things as they really are, for not being made a dupe of, not being taken in. But partly, also, a Liberal of the future may do it for the sake of his young Liberal friends, who, though they have committed themselves to the stream of the Liberalism which now is, are yet aware, many of them, of a great need for finding the passage from this Liberalism to the Liberalism of the future. And, although the passage is not easy to find, yet some of them perhaps, as they are men of admirable parts and energy, if only they see clearly the matters with which they have to deal, by a happy and divine inspiration may find it.

Let me begin by making myself as pleasant as I can to our Liberal friends, and by conceding to them that their recent triumph over their adversaries was natural and salutary. They reproach me, sometimes, with having drawn the picture of the Radical and Dissenting Bottles, but left the Tory Bottles unportrayed. Yet he exists, they urge, and is very baneful; and his ignoble Toryism it is, the shoddy Toryism of the City and of the Stock-Exchange, and not, as pompous leading-articles say, the intelligence and sober judgment of the educated classes and of mercantile sagacity, which carried the elections in the City of London and in the metropolitan counties for the Conservatives. Profoundly congenial to this shoddy Toryism,—so my Liberal reprovers go on to declare,—were the fashions and policy of Lord Beaconsfield, a policy flashy, insincere, immoral, worshipping material success above everything; profoundly congenial and profoundly demoralising. Now, I will not say that I adopt all these forcible and picturesque expressions of my Liberal friends, but I fully concede to them that although it is with the Radical and Dissenting Bottles that I have occupied myself,—for indeed he interests me far more than the other,—yet the Tory Bottles exists too, exists in great numbers and great force, particularly in London and its neighbourhood; and that, for him, Lord Beaconsfield and Lord Beaconsfield's style of government were at once very attractive and very demoralising. This, however, is but a detail of a great question. In general, the mind of the country is, as I have already said, profoundly Liberal; and it is Liberal by a just instinct. It feels that the Tories have not the secret of life and of the future for us, and it is right in so thinking. It turns to the Tories from time to time, in dissatisfaction at the shortcomings of Liberal statesmanship; but its reaction and recoil from them, after it has tried them for a little, is natural and salutary. For they cannot really profit the nation, or give it what it needs.

Moreover, we will concede, likewise, that what seems to many people the most dubious part of the Liberal programme, what is blamed as revolutionary and a leap in the dark, what is deprecated even by some of the most intelligent of Liberal statesmen as unnecessary and dangerous,—the proposal to give a vote to the agricultural labourer,—we will concede that this, too, is a thing not to be lamented and blamed, but natural and salutary. Not that there is either any natural right in every man to the possession of a vote, or any gift of wisdom and virtue conferred by such possession. But if experience has established any one thing in this world, it has estabblished this : that it is well for any great class and description of men in society to be able to say for itself what it wants, and not to have other classes, the so-called educated and intelligent classes, acting for it as its proctors, and supposed to understand its wants and to provide for them. They do not really understand its wants, they do not really provide for them. A class of men may often itself not either fully understand its own wants, or adequately express them; but it has a nearer interest and a more sure diligence in the matter than any of its proctors, and therefore a better chance of success. Let the agricultural labourer become articulate, let him speak for himself. In his present case we have the last left of our illusions, that one class is capable of properly speaking for another, answering for another; and it is an illusion like the rest.

All this we may be quite prepared to concede to the Liberalism which now is: the fitness and naturalness of the most disputed article in its programme, the fitness and naturalness of its adversaries' recent defeat. And yet, at the same time, what strikes one fully as much as all this, is the insecureness of the Liberals' hold upon office and upon public favour; the probability of the return, perhaps even more than once, of their adversaries to office, before that final and happy consummation is reached,—the permanent establishment of Liberalism in power.

Many people will tell us that this is because the multitude, by whose votes the elections are now decided, is ignorant and capricious and unstable, and gets tired of those who have been managing its affairs for some time, and likes a change to something new, and then gets tired of this also, and changes back again; and that so we may expect to go on changing from a Conservative government to a Liberal, and from a Liberal government to a Conservative, backwards and forwards for ever. But this is not so. Instinctively, however slowly, the human spirit struggles towards the light; and the adoptions and rejections of its agents by the multitude are never wholly blind and capricious, but have a meaning. And the Liberals of the future are those who preserve themselves from distractions and keep their heads as clear and their tempers as calm as they can, in order that they may discern this meaning; and therefore the Liberals of the present, who are too heated and busy to discern it, cannot do without them altogether, greatly as they are inclined to disregard them, but they have an interest in their cogitations whether they will or no.

What, then, is the meaning of the veerings of public favour from one of the two great parties which administer our affairs to the other, and why is it likely that the gust of favour, by which the Liberals have recently benefited, will not be a steady and permanent wind to bear them for ever prosperously along? Well, the reason of it is very simple, but the simple reason of a thing is often the very last that we will consent to look at. But as the end and aim of all dialectics is, as by the great master of dialectics we have been most truly told, to help us to an answer to the question, how to live; so, beyond all doubt whatever, have politics too to deal with this same question and with the discovery of an answer to it. The true and noble science of politics is even the very chief of the sciences, because it deals with this question for the benefit of man not as an isolated creature, but in that state 'without which,' as Burke says, 'man could not by any possibility arrive at the perfection of which his nature is capable,'—for the benefit of man in society. Now of man in society the capital need is, that the whole body of society should come to live with a life worthy to be called *human*, and corresponding to man's true aspirations and powers. This, the humanisation of man in society, is civilisation. The aim for all of us is to promote it, and to promote it is above all the aim for the true politician.

Of these general propositions we none of us, probably, deny or question the truth, although we do not much attend to them in our practice of politics, but are concerned with points of detail. Neither will any man, probably, be disposed to deny that, the aim for all of us, and for the politician more especially, being to make civilisation pervasive and general, the necessary means towards civilisation may be said to be, first and foremost, expansion ; and then, the power of expansion being given, these other powers have to follow it and to find their account in it :—the power of conduct, the power of intellect and knowledge, the power of beauty, the power of social life and manners. These are the means towards our end, which is civilisation ; and the true politician, who wills the end, cannot but will the means also. And meanwhile, whether the politician wills them or not, there is an instinct in society pushing it to desire them and to tend to them, and making it dissatisfied when nothing is done for them, or when impediment and harm are offered to them ; and this instinct we call the instinct of self-preservation in humanity. So long as any of the means to civilisation are neglected, or have impediment and harm offered to them, men are always, whether consciously or no, in want of something which they have not; they can never be really at ease. At times they even get angrily dissatisfied with themselves, their condition, and their government, and seek restlessly for a change.

Expansion we were bound to put first among the means towards civilisation, because it is the basis which man's whole effort to civilise himself requires and presupposes. The instinct for expansion manifests itself conspicuously in the love of liberty, and every one knows how signally this love is exhibited in England. Now, the Liberals are pre-eminently the party appealing to the love of liberty, and therefore to the instinct for expansion. The Conservatives may say that they love liberty as much as the Liberals love it, and that for real liberty they do as much. But it is evident that they do not appeal so principally as the Liberals to the love of liberty, because their principal appeal is to the love of order, to the respect for what they call 'our traditional, existing social arrangements.' Order is a most excellent thing, and true liberty is impossible without it; but order is not in itself liberty, and an appeal to the love of order is not a direct appeal to the love of liberty, to the instinct for expansion. The great body of the community, therefore, in which the instinct for expansion works powerfully and spreads more and more, this great body feels that to its primary instinct, its instinct for expansion, the Liberals rather than the Conservatives make appeal. Consequently this great body tends, and must tend, to go with the Liberals. And this is what I meant by saying, even at the time when the late Government seemed strongest, that the country was profoundly Liberal. The instinct for expansion was still, I meant to say, the primary instinct in the great body of our community; and this instinct is in alliance with the Liberals, not with the Conservatives.

To enlarge and secure our existence by the conveniences of life is the object of trade; and the development of trade, like that of liberty, is due to the working in men of the natural instinct of expansion. And the turn for trade our nation has shown as signally as the turn for liberty; and of its instinct for expansion, in this line also, the Liberals, and not the Conservatives, have been the great favourers. The mass of the community, pushed by the instinct for expansion, sees in the Liberals the friends of trade as well as the friends of liberty.

And, in fact, Liberal statesmen like the present Lord

Derby (who well deserves, certainly, that among the Liberals, as he himself desires, we should count him), and Liberal orators like Mr. Bright, are continually appealing, when they address the public, either to the love of liberty or to the love of trade, and praising Liberalism for having favoured and helped the one or the other, and blaming Conservatism for having discouraged and checked them. When they make these appeals, when they distribute this praise and this blame, they touch a chord in the public mind which vibrates strongly in answer. What the Liberals have done for liberty, what the Liberals have done for trade, and how under this beneficent impulsion the greatness of England has arisen, the greatness which comes, as the hearer is told, from 'the cities you have built, the railroads you have made, the manufactures you have produced, the cargoes which freight the ships of the greatest mercantile navy the world has ever seen,'—this, together with the virtues of Nonconformity and of Nonconformists, and the demerits of the Tories, may be said, as I have often remarked, to be the never-failing theme of Mr. Bright's speeches; and his treatment of the theme is a never-failing source of excitement and delight to his hearers. And how skilfully and effectively did Lord Derby the other day, in a speech in the north of England, treat after his own fashion the same kind of theme, pitying the wretched Continent of Europe, given over to 'emperors, grand dukes, archdukes, field-marshals, and tremendous personages of that sort,' and extolling Liberal England, free from such incubuses, and enabled by that freedom to get 'its manufacturing industries developed,' and to let 'our characteristic qualities for industrial supremacy have play.' Lord Derby here, like Mr. Bright, appeals to the instinct for expansion manifesting itself in our race by the love of liberty and the love of trade ; and to such a call, so effectively made, a popular audience in this country always responds.

What a source of strength is this for the Liberals, and how surely and abundantly do they profit by it ! Still, it is not all-sufficient. For we have working in us, as elements towards civilisation, besides the instinct for expansion, the instinct also, as was just now said, for conduct, the instinct for intellect and knowledge, the instinct for beauty, the instinct for a fit and pleasing form of social life and manners. And Lord Derby will allow, I am sure, when he thinks of St. Helens and of similar places, that even at his own gate, and amongst a population developing its manufacturing industries most fully, free from emperors and archdukes, congratulated by him on its freedom, and trade, and industrial supremacy, and responding joyfully to his congratulations, there is to be found, indeed, much satisfaction to the instinct in man for expansion, but little satisfaction to his instinct for beauty, and to his instinct for a fit and pleasing form of social life and manners. I will not at this moment speak of conduct, or of intellect and knowledge, because I wish to carry Lord Derby unhesitatingly with me in what I say. And certainly he will allow that the instinct of man for beauty, his instinct for fit and pleasing forms of social life and manners, is not well satisfied at St Helens. Cobbett, whom I have already quoted, used to call places of this kind *Hell-holes*. St. Helens is eminently what Cobbett meant by a *Hell-hole*, but it is only a type, however eminent, of a whole series of places so designated by him, such as Bolton, Wigan, and the like, places developing abundantly their manufacturing industries, but in which man's instinct for beauty, and man's instinct for fit and pleasing forms of social life and manners, in which these two instincts, at any rate, to say nothing for the present of others, find little or no satisfaction. Such places certainly must be said to show, in the words of a very different personage from Cobbett, the words of the accomplished President of the Royal Academy, Sir Frederick Leighton, 'no love of beauty, no sense of the outward dignity and comeliness of things calling on the part of the public for expression, and, as a corollary, no dignity, no comeliness, for the most part, in their outward aspect.'

And not only have the inhabitants of what Cobbett called a Hell-hole, and what Lord Derby and Mr. Bright would call a centre of manufacturing industry, no satisfaction of man's instinct for beauty to make them happy, but even their manufacturing industries they develope in such a manner, that from the exercise of this their instinct for expansion they do not procure the result which they expected, but they find uneasiness and stoppage. For in general they develope their industries in this wise : they produce, not something which it is very difficult to make, and of which people can never have enough, and which they themselves can make far better than anybody else ; but they produce that which is not hard to make, and of which there may easily be produced more than is wanted, and which more and more people, in different quarters, fall to making, as time goes on, for themselves, and which they soon make quite as well as the others do. But at a given moment, when there is a demand, or a chance of demand, for their manufacture, the capitalists in the *Hell-holes*, as Cobbett would say, or the leaders of industrial enterprise, as Lord Derby and Mr. Bright would call them, set themselves to produce as much as ever they can, without asking themselves how long the demand may last, so that it do but last long enough for them to make their own fortunes by it, or without thinking, in any way beyond this, about what they are doing, or troubling themselves any further with the future. And clusters and fresh clusters of men and women they collect at places like St. Helens and Bolton to manufacture for them, and call them into being there just as much as if they had begotten them. Then the demand ceases or slackens, because more has been produced than was wanted, or because people who used to come to us for the thing we produced take to producing it for themselves, and think that they can make it (and we have premised that it is a thing not difficult to make) quite as well as we can; or even, since some of our heroes of industrial enterprise have been in too great haste to make their fortunes, and unscrupulous in their processes, better. And perhaps these capitalists have had time to make their fortunes; but meanwhile they have not made the fortunes of the clusters of men and women whom they have called into being to produce for them, and whom they have, as I said, as good as begotten. But these they leave to the chances of the future, and of the further development, as Lord Derby says, of great manufacturing industries. And so there arise periods of depression of trade, there arise complaints of over-production, uneasiness and distress at our centres of manufacturing industry. People then begin, even although their instinct for expansion, so far as liberty is concerned, may have received every satisfaction, they begin to discover, like those unionist workmen whose words Mr. John Morley quotes, that 'free political institutions do not guarantee the well-being of the toiling class.'

But we need not go to visit the places which Cobbett called Hell-holes, or travel so far as St. Helens, close by Lord Derby's gate at Knowsley, or so far as Bolton or Wigan. We Londoners need not go away from the place where our own daily business lies, and from London itself, in order to see how insufficient for man is our way of gratifying his instinct for expansion and this instinct alone, and what comes of trusting too much to what is thus done for us. We have only to take the tramway at King's Cross, and to let ourselves be carried through Camden Town up the slopes towards Highgate and Hampstead, where from the upward-sloping ground, as we ascend, we have a good view all about us, and can survey much of human haunt and habitation. And in the pleasant season of the year, and in this humid and verdure-nursing English climate, we shall see plenty of flowering trees, and grass, and vegetation of all kinds to delight our eyes; but they will meet with nothing else to delight them. All that man has made there for his habitation and functions is singularly dull and mean, and does indeed, as we gradually mount the disfigured slopes and see it clearer and clearer, 'reveal the spectacle,' as Sir Frederick Leighton says, 'of the whole current of human life setting resolutely in a direction opposed to artistic production; no love of beauty, no sense of the outward dignity of things, and, as a corollary, no dignity, no comeliness, for the most part, in their outward aspect.' And here, in what we see from the tramway, we have a type, not of life at a centre of manufacturing industry, but of the life in general of the English middle class. We have the life of a class which has been able to follow freely its instinct of expansion, so far as to preserve itself from emperors and archdukes and tremendous personages of that sort, and to enjoy abundance of political liberty and of trade. But man's instinct for beauty has been maltreated and starved, in this class, in the manner we see. And man's instinct, also, for intellect and knowledge has been maltreated and starved; because the schools for this class, where it should have called forth and trained this instinct, are the worst of the kind anywhere. And the provision made by this class for the instinct which desires fit and pleasing forms of social life and manners is what might be expected from its provision for the instinct of beauty, and for the instinct leading us to intellect and knowledge.

But there this class lives, busy and confident ; and enjoys the amplest political liberty, and takes what Mr. Bright calls 'a commendable interest in politics,' and reads, what he says is such admirable reading for all of us, the newspapers. And thus there arises a type of life and opinion which that acute and powerful personage, Prince Bismarck, has described so excellently, that I cannot do better than use his words. 'When great numbers of people of this sort,' says Prince Bismarck, 'live close together, individualities naturally fade out and melt into each other. All sorts of opinions grow out of the air, from hearsays and talk behind people's backs ; opinions with little or no foundation in fact, but which get spread abroad through newspapers, popular meetings, and talk, and get themselves established and are ineradicable. People talk themselves into believing the thing that is not ; consider it a duty and obligation to adhere to their belief, and excite themselves about prejudices and absurdities.' Who does not recognise the truth of this account of *public opinion*,—public opinion in politics, public opinion in religion,—as it forms itself amongst such a description of people as the people through whose seats of habitation the tramway northward from King's

Cross takes us ; nay, as it forms itself amongst the English middle class in general, amongst the great community which we call that of the Philistines?

Now, this great Philistine community it is, with its liberty and its publicity, and its trade, and its love of all the three, but with its narrow range of intellect and knowledge, its stunted sense of beauty and dignity, its low standard of social life and manners, and its ignorance of its own deficiencies in respect of all these,—this Philistine middle class it is, to which a Liberal government has especially to make appeal, and on which it relies for support. And where such a government deals with foreign affairs, and addresses foreign nations, this is the force which it is known to have behind it, and to be forced to reckon with ; this class trained as we have seen, and with habits of thought and opinion formed as Prince Bismarck describes. It is this Englishman of the middle class, this Philistine with his likes and dislikes, his effusion and confusion, his hot fits and cold fits, his want of dignity and of the steadfastness which comes from dignity, his want of ideas, and of the steadfastness which comes from ideas, on whom a Liberal Foreign Minister must lean for support, and whose dispositions he must in great measure follow. Mr. Grant Duff and others are fond of sketching out a line of foreign policy which they say is the line of Liberal foreign policy, or of insisting on the dignity and ability of this or that Liberal statesman, such as Lord Granville, who may happen to hold the post of Foreign Minister. No one will wish to deny the dignity and ability of Lord Granville; and no one doubts that Mr. Grant Duff and his intelligent friends can easily draw out a striking and able line of foreign policy, and may call it the line of Liberal foreign policy if they please. But the real Liberal Foreign Minister, and the real Liberal foreign policy, are not to be looked for in Lord Granville left to himself, or in a programme drawn up in Mr. Grant Duff's library by himself and his intelligent friends; they receive a bias from the temper and thoughts, and from the hot fits and cold fits, of that middle class on which a Liberal government leans for support. And so we get such mortifications as those which befell us in the case of Prussia's dealing with Denmark and of Russia's dealing with the Black Sea; and foreign statesmen, knowing how the matter stands with us, say coolly what Dr. Busch reports Prince Bismarck to have said concerning a firm and dignified declaration by our Liberal Foreign Secretary: 'What does it matter? Nothing is to be feared, as nothing is to be hoped, from these people.'

Thus it happens that we suffer 'a loss of prestige,' as

it is called ; and we become aware of it, and then we are vexed and dissatisfied. Just as by following, as we do, our instinct for expansion, and by procuring the amplest political liberty and free trade, and by preserving ourselves from such tremendous personages as emperors, grand dukes, and archdukes, we yet do not preserve ourselves from depression of trade, so neither do we by all these advantages preserve ourselves from loss of prestige. And at this from time to time the public mind, as we all know, gets vexed and dissatisfied.

And other occasions of dissatisfaction, too, there may easily be, and at one or other of them there may be a veering round to the Tories, to see if they, perhaps, can do us any good. Now, we must remember in what case the great body of our community is, when it thus turns to the Tories in the hope of bettering itself. It has so far followed its instinct for expansion, to which Liberal statesmen make special appeal, as to obtain full political liberty and free trade. How far it has followed its instinct for conduct I will not now enquire ; the enquiry might lead us into a discussion of the whole condition of morals and religion in this nation. However, we may certainly say, I think, that in no country has the instinct for conduct been more followed than in our country, in few countries has it been followed so much. But the need of man for intellect and knowledge has not in the great body of our community been much attended to, nor have Liberal statesmen made much appeal to it. For giving the rudiments and instruments of knowledge to the lowest class amongst us they have, indeed, sought of late to make provision, but for the advancement of intellect and knowledge among the middle classes they have made little or none. The need of man for beauty, again, has been by the great body of our community scarcely at all heeded, neither have Liberal statesmen sought to appeal to it. Of the need of man for fit and pleasing forms of social life and manners we may say the same.

In this position are things, when from time to time the great body of our community turns to the Conservatives, or, as they are now beginning to be called again, the Tories, in the hope of bettering itself. Now, the need of man for expansion we are all agreed that Liberal statesmen, and not Tory statesmen, make appeal to, and that the great body of the community feels this need powerfully. But the other needs which it feels so little, and to which Liberal statesmen so little make appeal, are yet working obscurely in the community all the time, and craving for some notice and help, and begetting dissatisfaction with the sort of life which is the lot of man when they are utterly neglected.

So to the Tories, in some such moment of dissatisfaction, the community turns. Now, to the need in man for conduct we will not say that Tory statesmen make much appeal, for the upper class, to which they belong, is now, we know, in great measure materialised; and probably Mr. Jowett, who, though he is a man of integrity and a most honest translator, has yet his strokes of malice, had this in his mind, where he brings in his philosopher saying that 'the young men of the governing class are as indifferent as the pauper to the cultivation of virtue.' Yet so far as dignity is a part of conduct, an aristocratic class, trained to be sensitive on the point of honour, and to think much of the grandeur and dignity of their country, do appeal to the instinct in man for conduct; but perhaps dignity may more conveniently be considered here as a part of beauty than as a part of conduct. Therefore to the need for beauty, starved by those who, —following the hot and cold fits of the opinion of a middle class testy, ignorant, a little ignoble, unapt to perceive when it is making itself ridiculous,—may have brought about for our country a loss of *prestige*, as it is called, and of the respect of foreign nations, to this need Tory statesmen, leaning upon the opinion of an aristocratic class by nature more firm, reticent, dignified, sensitive on the point of honour, do, I think, give some satisfaction. And the aristocratic class, of which they are the agents, give some satisfaction, moreover, to this baffled and starved instinct for beauty, by the spectacle of a splendour, and grace, and elegance of life, due to inherited wealth and to traditional refinement; and to the instinct for fit and seemly forms of social intercourse and manners they give some satisfaction too.

To the instinct for intellect and knowledge, however, the aristocratic class and its agents, the Tory statesmen, give no satisfaction at all. To large and clear ideas of the future and of its requirements, whether at home or abroad, aristocracies are by nature inaccessible; and though the firmness and dignity of their carriage, in foreign affairs, may inspire respect and give satisfaction, yet even here, as they do not see how the world is really going, they can found nothing. By the possession of what is beautiful in outward life, and of what is seemly in manners, they do, as we have seen, attract; but for the active communication and propagation, all through the community, of what is beautiful in outward life, and of what is seemly in manners, they do next to nothing. And, finally, to the instinct in the great body of the community for expansion they are justly felt to be even adverse, in so far as the very first consideration with them as a class,—a few humane individuals amongst them, lovers of perfection, being left out of account,—is always 'the maintenance of our traditional, existing social arrangements.'

Consequently, however public favour may have veered round to them for a time, it soon appears that they cannot satisfy the needs of the community, and the turn of the Liberal statesmen comes again. Such a turn came to them not long ago. And the danger is, that the Liberal statesmen should again do only what it is easy and natural to them to do, because they have done it so often and so successfully already,—appeal vigorously to the love of political liberty and to the love of trade, and lean mainly upon the opinion of the middle class, as this class now is, and do nothing to make it sounder and better by appealing to the sense, in the body of the community, for intellect and knowledge, and striving to call it forth, and by appealing to the sense for beauty and to the sense for manners; and by appealing, moreover, to the sense for expansion more wisely and fruitfully than they do now. But if they do nothing of this kind, and simply return to their old courses, then there will inevitably be, after a while, pressure and stoppage and reproaches and dissatisfaction, and the turn of the Tories will come round again. Who knows?—some day, perhaps, even the Liberal panacea of sheer political liberty may be for a time discredited, and the fears of 'Verax' about personal government may come true, and the last scene in the wonderful career of Lord Beaconsfield may be that we shall see him, in a field marshal's uniform, entering the House of Commons, and pointing to the mace, and commanding Lord Rowton, in an octogenarian voice, to 'take away that bauble.' But still the rule of the Tories, even after such a masterstroke as that, will never last in our community; such strangers are the Tory statesmen to the secret of our community's life, to the secret of the future.

Only let Liberal statesmen, at their returns to power, instead of losing themselves in the petty bustle and schemes of the moment, bethink themselves what that aim of the community's life really is, and that secret of the life of the future: that it is civilisation, and civilisation made pervasive and general. Hitherto our Liberal statesmen themselves have conceived that aim very imperfectly, and very imperfectly worked for it, and this although they are called the leaders of progress. Hence the instability of their government, and the veerings round of public favour, now and again, to their adversaries. I have said that with one great element of civilisation, the instinct in the community for expansion, Liberal statesmen are in alliance, and that their strength is due to that cause. Of the instinct for conduct I have said that we will not here speak ; it might lead us too far, and into the midst of matters of which I have spoken enough formerly, and of which I wish, as far as possible, to renounce the discussion. But for the other means of civilisation Liberal statesmen really do little or nothing ; and this explains their instability. Let us not cover up their shortcomings, but rather draw them into light. For the need of intellect and knowledge what do they do? They will point to elementary education. But elementary education goes so little way, that in giving it one hardly does more than satisfy man's instinct for expansion, one scarcely satisfies his need of intellect and knowledge at all; any more than the achievement of primitive man in providing himself with his simple working tools is a satisfying of the human need for intellect and knowledge. For the need of beauty Liberal statesmen do nothing, for the need of manners nothing. And they lean especially upon the opinion of one great class,—the middle class,—with virtues of its own, indeed, but at the same time full of narrowness, full of prejudices ; with a defective type of religion, a narrow range of intellect and knowledge, a stunted sense of beauty, a low standard of manners ; and averse, moreover, to whatever may disturb it in its vulgarity. How can such statesmen be said, any more than the Tories, to grasp that idea of civilisation which is the secret of the life of our community and of the life of the future?—to grasp the idea fully, and with potent effect to work for it?

We who now talk of these things shall be in our graves long before Liberal statesmen can have entirely mended their ways, and set themselves steadily to bring about the reign of a civilisation pervasive and general. But a beginning towards it they may make even now, and perhaps they are making it. Perhaps Liberal statesmen are beginning to see what they have lost by following too submissively middle-class opinion hitherto, our middle class being such as it is now; and they may be resolving to avoid for the future this cause of mischief to them. Perhaps Lord Granville is bent on planning and maintaining a line of foreign policy, such as a man of his means of information and of his insight and high feeling can well devise, and such as Mr. Grant Duff is always telling us that the real line of Liberal foreign policy is; perhaps Lord Granville is even now ready with a policy of this sort, and resolved to adhere to it whatever may be in the meanwhile the hot fits and the cold fits, the effusion and confusion, of the British Philistine of the middle class. Perhaps Liberal statesmen have made up their minds no longer to govern Ireland in deference to the narrow prejudices and antipathies of this class. And perhaps, as time goes on, they will even turn resolutely round and look their middle-class friends full in the face, and tell them of their imperfections, and try to cure them.

And then Lord Derby, when he speaks at St. Helens or at some other place like it, will not extol his hearers as 'an intelligent, keen-witted, critical, and well-to-do population such as our northern towns in England show,' but he will point out to them that they have a defective type of religion, a narrow range of intellect and knowledge, a stunted sense of beauty, a low standard of manners; and that they prove it by having made St. Helens, and by the life which they lead there ; and that they ought to do better. And Mr. Bright, instead of telling his Islington Nonconformists 'how much of what there is free and good and great in England, and constantly growing in what is good, is owing to Nonconformist action,' will rather admonish them that the Puritan type of life exhibits a religion not true, the claims of intellect and knowledge not satisfied, the claim of beauty not satisfied, the claim of manners not satisfied; and that if, as he says, the lower classes in this country have utterly abandoned the dogmas of Christianity, and the upper classes its practice, the cause lies very much in the impossible and unlovely presentment of Christian dogmas and practice which is offered by the most important part of this nation, the serious middle class, and above all by its Nonconforming portion. And, since the failure here in civilisation comes not from an insufficient care for political liberty and for trade, nor yet from an insufficient care for conduct, but from an insufficient care for intellect and knowledge and beauty and a humane life, let Liberal statesmen despise and neglect for the cure of our present imperfection no means, whether of public schools, now wanting, or of the theatre, now left to itself and to chance, or of anything else which may powerfully conduce to the communication and propagation of real intelligence, and of real beauty, and of a life really humane.

Objects which Liberal statesmen pursue now, and which are not in themselves ends of civilisation, they may possibly have to pursue still; but let them pursue them in a different spirit. For instance, there are those well-known Liberal objects, that of legalising marriage with a deceased wife's sister, that of permitting Dissenters to use what burial-services they like in the parish church-yard, and that of granting what is termed Local Option. Every one of these objects may be attained, and it may even be necessary to attain them, and yet, after they are attained, the imperfections of our civilisation will stand just as they did before, and the real work of Liberal statesmen will have yet to begin.

Some Liberals misconceive the character of these

objects strangely. Mr. Bright urges Parliament to pass the Bill legalising marriage with a deceased wife's sister, in order that Parliament may 'affirm by an emphatic vote the principle of personal liberty for the men and women of this country in the chief concern of their lives.' But the whole institution and sacredness of marriage is an abridgment of the principle of personal liberty in the concern in question. When Herod the tetrarch wanted to marry Herodias, his brother Philip's wife, he was seeking to affirm emphatically the principle of personal liberty in the concern of his marriage; and we all know him to have been doing wrong. Every limitation of choice in marriage is an abridgment of the principle of personal liberty; but there needs more delicacy of perception, more civilisation, to understand and accept the abridgment in some cases than in others. Very many in the lower class in this country, and many in the middle class,—the civilisation and the capacity for delicate perception in these classes being what they are,—fail to understand and accept the prohibition to marry their deceased wife's sister. That they ought not to marry their brother's wife they can perceive; that they ought not to marry their wife's sister they cannot. And so they contract these marriages freely, and the evil of their freely committing a breach of the law may be more than the good of imposing on them a restriction, which in their present state they have not perception enough to understand and obey. Therefore it may be expedient to legalise, amongst our people, marriage with a deceased wife's sister. Still, our civilisation, which it is the end of the true and noble science of politics to perfect, gains thereby hardly anything; and of its continued imperfection, indeed, the very call for the Bill in question is a proof.

So, again, with measures like that for granting Local Option, as it is called, for doing away the addiction of our lower class to their porter and their gin. It is necessary to do away their addiction to these; and, for that end, to receive at the hands of the friends of temperance some such measure as the Bill for granting Local Option. Yet the alimentary secret of the life of civilised man is by no means possessed by the friends of temperance as we now see them either here or in America; and whoever has been amongst the population of the Médoc district, in France, will surely feel, if he is not a fanatic, that the civilised man of the future is more likely to adopt their beverage than to eat and drink like Dr. Richardson.

And so too, again, with the Burials Bill. It is a Bill for enabling the Dissenters to use their own burial services in the parish churchyard. Now, we all know what the services of many of the Protestant Dissenters are; and that whereas the burial service of the Church of England may be compared, as I have said somewhere or other, to a reading from Milton, so a burial service, such as pleases many of the Protestant Dissenters, may be likened to a reading from Eliza Cook. But fractious clergymen could refuse, as is well known, to give their reading from Milton, or any reading at all, over the children of Baptists; and the remedy for this was to abolish the rubric giving them the power of such refusal. The clergy, however, as if to prove the truth of Clarendon's sentence on them, a sentence which should be written up over the portal of the Lower House of Convocation : ' *Clergymen, who understand the least, and take the worst measure of human affairs, of all mankind that can write and read!*' —the clergy, it seems, had rather the world should go to pieces than that this rubric should be abolished. And so Liberal statesmen must pass the Burials Bill ;—for it is better even to have readings from Eliza Cook in the parish churchyard, than to have fractious clergymen armed with the power of refusing to bury the children of Baptists. Still, our civilisation is not really advanced by any such measure as the Burials Bill ; nay, in so far as readings from Eliza Cook are encouraged to produce themselves in public, and to pass themselves off as equivalent to readings from Milton, it is retarded.

Therefore do not let Liberal statesmen estimate the

so-called Liberal measures, many of them, which they may be called upon to recommend now, at more than they are worth, or suppose that by recommending them they at all remedy their shortcomings in the past ;—shortcomings which consist in their having taken an incomplete view of the life of the community and of its needs, and in having done little or nothing for the need of intellect and knowledge, and for the need of beauty, and for the need of manners, but having thought it enough to work for political liberty and free trade, for the need of expansion.

Nay, but even for the need of expansion our Liberal statesmen have not worked adequately. Doubtless the need of expansion in men suffers a defeat when they are over-tutored, over-governed, *sat upon*, as we say, by authority military or civil. From such a defeat of our instinct for expansion, political liberty saves us Englishmen; and Liberal statesmen have worked for political liberty. But the need of expansion suffers a defeat, also, wherever there is an immense inequality of conditions and property; such inequality inevitably depresses and degrades the inferior masses. And whenever any great need of human nature suffers defeat, then the nation, in which the defeat happens, finds difficulties befalling it from that cause; nay, and the victories of other great needs do not compensate for the defeat of one. Germany, where the need for intellect and science is well cared for, where the sense of conduct is strong, has neither liberty nor equality; the instinct for expansion suffers there signal defeat. Hence the difficulties of Germany. France has liberty and equality, the instinct for expansion is victorious there; but how greatly does the need for conduct suffer defeat! and hence the difficulties of France. We English people have, deep and strong, the sense of conduct, and we have half of the instinct for expansion fully satisfied;—that is to say, we have admirable political liberty, and we have free trade. But we have inequality rampant, and hence arise many of our difficulties.

For in honest truth our present state, as I have elsewhere said, may without any great injustice be summed up thus: that we have an upper class materialised, a middle class vulgarised, a lower class brutalised. And this we owe to our inequality. For, if Lord Derby would think of it, he is himself at Knowsley quite as tremendous a personage, over against St. Helens, as the emperors and grand dukes and archdukes who fill him with horror. And though he himself may be one of the humane few who emerge in all classes, and may have escaped being materialised, yet still, owing to his tremendousness, the middle class of St. Helens is thrown in upon itself, and not civilised; and the lower class, again, is thrown in upon itself, and not civilised. And some who fill the place which he now fills are certain to be, some of them, materialised;—like his great-grandfather, for instance, whose cock-fights, as it is said, are still remembered with gratitude and love by old men in Preston. And he himself, being so able and acute as he is, would never, if he were not in a false position and compelled by it to use unreal language, he would never talk so much to his hearers, in the towns of the north, about their being 'an intelligent, keen-witted, critical, and well-to-do population;' but he would reproach them, though kindly and mildly, for having made St. Helens and places like it, and he would exhort them to civilise themselves.

But of inequality, as a defeat to the instinct in the community for expansion, and as a sure cause of trouble, Liberal statesmen are very shy to speak. And in Ireland, where inequality and the system of great estates produces, owing to differences of religion, and to absenteeism, and to the ways of personages such as the late Lord Leitrim, even more tremendous, perhaps, than an emperor or an archduke, and to the whole history of the country and character of the people,—in Ireland, I say, where inequality produces, owing to all these, more pressing and evident troubles than in England, and is the second cause of our difficulties with the Irish, as the habit of governing them in deference to British middle-class prejudices is the first,—in Ireland Liberal statesmen never look the thing fairly in the face, or apply a real remedy, but invent palliatives like the Irish Land Act, which do not go to the root of the evil, but which unsettle men's notions as to the constitutive characters of property, making these characters something quite different in one place from what they are in another. And in England, where inequality and the system of great estates produces trouble too, though not trouble so glaring as in Ireland, in England Liberal statesmen shrink even more from looking the thing in the face, and apply little palliatives; and even for these little palliatives they allege reasons which are extremely questionable, such as that each child has a natural right to his equal share of his father's property, or that land in the hands of many owners will certainly produce more than in the hands of few. And the true and simple reason against inequality they avert their eyes from, as if it were a Medusa;—the reason, namely, that inequality, in a society like ours, sooner or later inevitably materialises the upper class, vulgarises the middle class, brutalises the lower class.

Not until this need to which they appeal, the need in

man for expansion, is better understood by Liberal statesmen, is understood to include equality as well as political liberty and free trade,—and is cared for by them, yet cared for not singly and exorbitantly, but in union and proportion with the progress of man in conduct, and his growth in intellect and knowledge, and his nearer approach to beauty and manners,—will Liberal governments be secure. But when Liberal statesmen have learned to care for all these together, and to go on unto perfection or true civilisation, then at last they will be professing and practising the true and noble science of politics and the true and noble science of economics, instead of, as now, semblances only of these sciences, or at best fragments of them. And then will come at last the extinction or the conversion of the Tories, the restitution of all things, the reign of the Liberal saints. But meanwhile, so long as the Liberals do only as they have done hitherto, they will not permanently satisfy the community; but the Tories will again, from time to time, be tried,—tried and found wanting. And we, who study to be quiet, and to keep our temper and our tongue under control, shall continue to speak of the principles of our two great political parties much as we do now; while clear-headed, but rough, impatient, and angry men, like Cobbett, will call them *the principles of Pratt, the principles of Yorke.*

A SPEECH AT ETON.[1]

THE philosopher Epictetus, who had a school at Nicopolis in Epirus at the end of the first century of our era, thus apostrophises a young gentleman whom he supposes to be applying to him for education :—

'Young sir, at home you have been at fisticuffs with the man-servant, you have turned the house upside down, you have been a nuisance to the neighbours; and do you come here with the composed face of a sage, and mean to sit in judgment upon the lesson, and to criticise my want of point? You have come in here with envy and chagrin in your heart, humiliated at not getting your allowance paid you from home; and you sit with your mind full, in the intervals of the lecture, of how your father behaves to you, and how your brother. What are the people down at home saying about me?—They are thinking: Now he is getting on! they are saying: He will come home a walking dictionary!—Yes, and I should

---

[1] Address delivered to the Eton Literary Society.

like to go home a walking dictionary; but then there is a deal of work required, and nobody sends me anything, and the bathing here at Nicopolis is dirty and nasty; things are all bad at home, and all bad here.'

Nobody can say that the bathing at Eton is dirty and nasty. But at Eton, as at Nicopolis, the moral disposition in which the pupil arrives at school, the thoughts and habits which he brings with him from home and from the social order in which he moves, must necessarily affect his power of profiting by what his schoolmasters have to teach him. This necessity is common to all schooling. You cannot escape from it here any more than they could at Nicopolis. Epictetus, however, was fully persuaded that what he had to teach was valuable, if the mental and moral frame of his pupils were but healthy enough to permit them to profit by it. I hope the Eton masters have the same conviction as to the native value of what they teach. But you know how many doubters and deniers of the value of a classical education we nowadays meet with. Let us put aside all that is said of the idleness, extravagance, and self-indulgence of the schoolboy. This may pair off with the complaint of Epictetus about the unsatisfactory moral state of his pupil. But with us there are many people who go on and say: 'And when the schoolboy, in our public schools, does learn, he learns nothing that is worth knowing.'

It is not of the Eton schoolboy only that this is said, but of the public schoolboy generally. We are all in the same boat,—all of us in whose schooling the Greek and Latin classics fill the principal place. And it avails nothing, that you try and appease the gainsayer by now acquainting yourselves with the diameter of the sun and moon, and with all sorts of matters which to us of an earlier and ruder generation were unknown. So long as the Greek and Latin classics continue to fill, as they do fill, the chief place in your school-work, the gainsayer is implacable and sticks to his sentence: 'When the boy does learn, he learns nothing that is worth knowing.'

Amidst all this disparagement, one may well ask oneself anxiously what is really to be said on behalf of studies over which so much of our time is spent, and for which we have, many of us, contracted a fondness. And after much consideration I have arrived at certain conclusions, which for my own use I find sufficient, but which are of such extreme simplicity that one ought to hesitate, perhaps, before one produces them to other people. However, such as they are, I have been led to bring them out more than once, and I will very briefly rehearse them now. It seems to me, firstly, that what a man seeks through his education is to get to know himself and the world; next, that for this knowledge it is before all things necessary that he acquaint himself with the best which has been thought and said in the world; finally, that of this *best* the classics of Greece and Rome form a very chief portion, and the portion most entirely satisfactory. With these conclusions lodged safe in one's mind, one is staunch on the side of the humanities.

And in the same spirit of simplicity in which these conclusions have been reached, I proceed further. People complain that the significance of the classics which we read at school is not enough brought out, that the whole order and sense of that world from which they issue is not seized and held up to view. Well, but the best, in literature, has the quality of being in itself formative,— silently formative; of bringing out its own significance as we read it. It is better to read a masterpiece much, even if one does that only, than to read it a little, and to be told a great deal about its significance, and about the development and sense of the world from which it issues. Sometimes what one is told about the significance of a work, and about the development of a world, is extremely questionable. At any rate, a schoolboy, who, as they did in the times of ignorance at Eton, read his Homer and Horace through, and then read them through again, and so went on until he knew them by heart, is not, in my opinion, so very much to be pitied.

Still that sounding phrase, 'the order and sense of a world,' sends a kind of thrill through us when we hear it, especially when the world spoken of is a thing so great and so interesting as the Græco-Roman world of antiquity. If we are not deluded by it into thinking that to read fine talk about our classical documents is as good as to read the documents themselves, the phrase is one which we may with advantage lay to heart. I remember being struck, long ago, with a remark on the Greek poet Theognis by Goethe, who did not know Greek well and had to pick out its meaning by the help of a Latin translation, but who brought to everything which he read his powerful habits of thought and criticism. 'When I first read Theognis,' says Goethe, in substance, 'I thought him querulous and morbid, and disliked him. But when I came to know how entirely his poetry proceeded from the real circumstances of his life, from the situation of parties in Megara, his native city, and from the effects of that situation upon himself and his friends, then I read him with quite another feeling.' How very little do any of us treat the poetry of Theognis and other ancients in that fashion ! was my thought after reading Goethe's criticism. And earlier still I remember being struck at hearing a schoolfellow, who had left the sixth form at Rugby for Cambridge, and who had fallen in somewhere with one of Bunsen's sons, who is now a member of the German Parliament,—at hearing this schoolfellow contrast the training of George Bunsen, as we then called him, with our own. Perhaps you think that at Rugby, which is often spoken of, though quite erroneously, as a sort of opposition establishment to Eton, we treated the classics in a high philosophical way, and traced the sequence of things in ancient literature, when you at Eton professed nothing of the kind. But hear the criticism of my old schoolfellow. 'It is wonderful,' said he; 'not only can George Bunsen construe his Herodotus, but he has a view of the place of Herodotus in literary history, a thing none of us ever thought about.' My friend spoke the truth; but even then, as I listened to him, I felt an emotion at hearing of the place of Herodotus in literary history. Yes, not only to be able to read the admirable works of classical literature, but to conceive also that Græco-Roman world, which is so mighty a factor in our own world, our own life, to conceive it as a whole of which we can trace the sequence, and the sense, and the connexion with ourselves, this does undoubtedly also belong to a classical education, rightly understood.

But even here, too, a plain person can proceed, if he

likes, with great simplicity. As Goethe says of life: Strike into it anywhere, lay hold of it anywhere, it is always powerful and interesting,—so one may almost say of classical literature. Strike into it where you like, lay hold of it where you like, you can nearly always find a thread which will lead you, if you follow it, to large and instructive results. Let us to-night follow a single Greek word in this fashion, and try to compensate ourselves, however imperfectly, for having to divert our thoughts, just for one evening's lecture, from the diameter of the sun and moon.

The word I will take is the word *eutrapelos, eutrapelia.* Let us consider it first as it occurs in the famous Funeral Oration put by Thucydides into the mouth of Pericles. The word stands there for one of the chief of those qualities which have made Athens, says Pericles, 'the school of Greece;' for a quality by which Athens is eminently representative of what is called Hellenism: the quality of flexibility. 'A happy and gracious flexibility,' Pericles calls this quality of the Athenians; and it is no doubt a charming gift. Lucidity of thought, clearness and propriety of language, freedom from prejudice and freedom from stiffness, openness of mind, amiability of manners, all these seem to go along with a certain happy flexibility of nature, and to depend upon it. Nor does this suppleness and flexibility of nature at all necessarily imply, as we English are apt to suppose, a relaxed moral fibre and weakness. In the Athenian of the best time it did not. 'In the Athenians,' says Professor Curtius, 'the sense of energy abhorred every kind of waste of time, their sense of measure abhorred bombast and redundancy, and their clear intelligence everything partaking of obscurity or vagueness; it was their habit in all things to advance directly and resolutely to the goal. Their dialect is characterised by a superior seriousness, manliness, and vigour of language.'

There is no sign of relaxation of moral fibre here ; and yet, at the same time, the Athenians were eminent for a happy and gracious flexibility. That quality, as we all know, is not a characteristic quality of the Germanic nations, to which we ourselves belong. Men are educable, and when we read of the abhorrence of the Attic mind for redundancy and obscurity of expression, its love for direct and telling speech, and then think of modern German, we may say with satisfaction that the circumstances of our life have at any rate educated us into the use of straightforward and vigorous forms of language. But they have not educated us into flexibility. All around us we may observe proofs of it. The state of

Ireland is a proof of it. We are rivals with Russia in Central Asia, and at this moment it is particularly interesting to note, how the want of just this one Athenian quality of flexibility seems to tell against us in our Asiatic rivalry with Russia. 'Russia,' observes one who is perhaps the first of living geographers,—an Austrian, Herr von Hellwald,—'possesses far more shrewdness, *flexibility*, and congeniality than England; qualities adapted to make the Asiatic more tractable.' And again : 'There can be no dispute which of the two, England or Russia, is the more civilised nation. But it is just as certain that the highly civilised English understand but indifferently how to raise their Asiatic subjects to their own standard of civilisation ; whilst the Russians attain, with their much lower standard of civilisation, far greater results amongst the Asiatic tribes, whom they know how to assimilate in the most remarkable manner. Of course they can only bring them to the same level which they have reached themselves ; but the little which they can and do communicate to them counts actually for much more than the great boons which the English do not know how to impart. Under the auspices of Russia the advance in civilisation amongst the Asiatics is indeed slow and inconsiderable, but steady, and suitable to their natural capacities and the disposition of their race. On the other hand, they remain indifferent to British civilisation, which is absolutely incomprehensible to them.'

Our word 'flexibility' has here carried us a long way, carried us to Turkestan and the valleys of the Jaxartes and Oxus. Let us get back to Greece, at any rate. The generation of Pericles is succeeded by the generation of Plato and Aristotle. Still the charming and Athenian quality of *eutrapelia* continues to be held in high esteem. Only the word comes to stand more particularly for flexibility and felicity in the give-and-take of gay and light social intercourse. With Aristotle it is one of the virtues: the virtue of him who in this pleasant sort of intercourse, so relished by the Greeks, manages exactly to hit the happy and right mean; the virtue opposed to buffoonery on the one side, and to morose rusticity, or clownishness, on the other. It is in especial the virtue of the young, and is akin to the grace and charm of youth. When old men try to adapt themselves to the young, says Plato, they betake themselves, in imitation of the young, to *eutrapelia* and pleasantry.

Four hundred years pass, and we come to the date of the Epistle to the Ephesians. The word *eutrapelia* rises in the mind of the writer of that Epistle. It rises to St. Paul's mind, and he utters it; but in how different a sense from the praising and admiring sense in which we have seen the word used by Thucydides and Aristotle! *Eutrapelia*, which once stood for that eminently Athenian and Hellenic virtue of happy and gracious flexibility, now conveys this favourable sense no longer, but is ranked, with filthiness and foolish talking, among things which are not convenient. Like these, it is not to be even so much as once named among the followers of God: 'neither filthiness, nor foolish talking, nor jesting (*eutrapelia*), which are not convenient.'

This is an extraordinary change, you will say. But now, as we have descended four hundred years from Aristotle to St. Paul, let us ascend, not four hundred, not quite even one hundred years, from Thucydides to Pindar. The religious Theban poet, we shall see (and the thing is surely very remarkable), speaks of the quality of *eutrapelia* in the same disapproving and austere way as the writer of the Epistle to the Ephesians. The young and noble Jason appears at Iolcos, and being questioned about himself by Pelias, he answers that he has been trained in the nurture and admonition of the old and just Centaur, Chiron. 'From his cave I come, from Chariclo and Philyra, his stainless daughters, who there nursed me. Lo, these twenty years am I with them, and there hath been found in me neither deed nor word that is not convenient; and now, behold, I am come home, that I may recover my father's kingdom.' The adjective *eutrapelos*, as it is here used in connexion with its two nouns, means exactly a word or deed, in Biblical phrase, *of vain lightness*, a word or deed *such as is not convenient*.

There you have the history of the varying use of the words *eutrapelos, eutrapelia*. And now see how this varying use gives us a clue to the order and sense, as we say, of all that Greek world, so nearly and wonderfully connected with us, so profoundly interesting for us, so full of precious lessons.

We must begin with generalities, but we will try not to lose ourselves in them, and not to remain amongst them long. Human life and human society arise, we know, out of the presence in man of certain needs, certain instincts, and out of the constant endeavour of these instincts to satisfy and develope themselves. We may briefly sum them up, these needs or instincts, as being, first and foremost, a general instinct of expansion; then, as being instincts following diverse great lines, which may be conveniently designated as the lines of conduct, of intellect and knowledge, of beauty, of social life and manners. Some lines are more in view and more in honour at one time, some at another. Some men and some nations are more eminent on one line, some on another. But the final aim, of making our own and of harmoniously combining the powers to be reached on each and all of these great lines, is the ideal of human life. And our race is for ever recalled to this aim, and held fast to it, by the instinct of self-preservation in humanity.

The ideal of human life being such as it is, all these great and diverse powers, to the attainment of which our instincts, as we have seen, impel us, hang together,—cannot be truly possessed and employed in isolation. Yet it is convenient, owing to the way in which we find them actually exhibiting themselves in human life and in history, to treat them separately, and to make distinctions of rank amongst them. In this view, we may say that the power of conduct is the greatest of all the powers now named; that it is even three-fourths of life. And wherever much is founded amongst men, there the power of conduct has surely been present and at work, although of course there may be and are, along with it, other powers too.

Now, then, let us look at the beginnings of that Greece to which we owe so much, and which we may almost, so far as our intellectual life is concerned, call the mother of us all. 'So well has she done her part,' as the Athenian Isocrates truly says of her, 'that the name of Greeks seems no longer to stand for a race, but to stand for intelligence itself; and they who share in

Hellenic culture are called Greeks even before those who are merely of Hellenic blood.' The beginnings of this wonderful Greece, what are they?

Greek history begins for us with the sanctuaries of Tempe and Delphi, and with the Apolline worship and priesthood which in those sanctuaries under Olympus and Parnassus established themselves. The northern sanctuary of Tempe soon yielded to Delphi as the centre of national Hellenic life and of Apolline religion. We are accustomed to think of Apollo as the awakener and nourisher of what is called genius, and so from the very first the Greeks, too, considered him. But in those earliest days of Hellas, and at Delphi, where the hardy and serious tribes of the Dorian highlands made their influence felt, Apollo was not only the nourisher of genius, he was also the author of every higher moral effort. He was the prophet of his father Zeus, in the highest view of Zeus, as the source of the ideas of moral order and of right. For to this higher significance had the names of Zeus and Phœbus,—names originally derived from sun and air,—gradually risen. They had come to designate a Father, the source of the ideas of moral order and of right; and a Son, his prophet, purifying and inspiring the soul with these ideas, and also with the idea of intellectual beauty.

Now, the ideas of moral order and of right which are in human nature, and which are, indeed, a main part of human life, were especially, we are told, a treasure possessed by the less gay and more solitary tribes in the mountains of Northern Greece. These Dorian tribes were Delphi's first pupils. And the graver view of life, the thoughts which give depth and solemnity to man's consciousness, the moral ideas, in short, of conduct and righteousness, were the governing elements in the manner of spirit propagated from Delphi. The words written up on the temple at Delphi called all comers to *soberness and righteousness*. The Doric and Æolic Pindar felt profoundly this severe influence of Delphi. It is not to be considered as an influence at war with the idea of intellectual beauty;—to mention the name of Pindar is in itself sufficient to show how little this was, or could be, the case. But it was, above all, an influence charged with the ideas of moral order and of right.

And there were confronting these Dorian founders of Hellas, and well known to them, and connected with them in manifold ways, other Greeks of a very different spiritual type; the Asiatic Greeks of Ionia, full of brilliancy and mobility, but over whom the ideas of moral order and of right had too little power, and who could never succeed in founding among themselves a serious and powerful state. It was evident that the great source of the incapacity which accompanied, in these Ionians of Asia, so much brilliancy, that the great enemy in them to the *Halt*, as Goethe calls it, the steadiness, which moral natures so highly prize, was their extreme mobility of spirit, their gay lightness, their *eutrapelia*. For Pindar, therefore, the word *eutrapelos*, expressing easy flexibility and mobility, becomes a word of stern opprobrium, and conveys the reproach of vain folly.

The Athenians were Ionians. But they were Ionians transplanted to Hellas, and who had breathed, as a Hellenic nation, the air of Delphi, that bracing atmosphere of the ideas of moral order and of right. In this atmosphere the Athenians, Ionian as they were, imbibed influences of character and steadiness, which for a long while balanced their native vivacity and mobility, distinguished them profoundly from the Ionians of Asia, and gave them men like Aristides.

Still, the Athenians were Ionians. They had the Ionian quickness and flexibility, the Ionian turn for gaiety, wit, and fearless thinking, the Ionian impatience of restraint. This nature of theirs asserted itself, first of all, as an impatience of *false* restraint. It asserted itself in opposition to the real faults of the Dorian spirit,—faults which became more and more manifest as time went on to the unprogressiveness of this spirit, to its stiffness, hardness, narrowness, prejudice, want of insight, want of amiability. And in real truth, by the time of Pericles, Delphi, the great creation of the Dorian spirit, had broken down, and was a witness to that spirit's lack of a real power of life and growth. Bribes had discredited the sanctity of Delphi; seriousness and vital power had left it. It had come to be little more than a name, and what continued to exist there was merely a number of forms.

Now then was the turn of the Athenians. With the idea of conduct, so little grasped by the Ionians of Asia, still deeply impressed on their soul, they freely and joyfully called forth also that pleasure in life, that love of clear thinking and of fearless discussion, that gay social temper, that ease and lightness, that gracious flexibility, which were in their nature. These were their gifts, and they did well to bring them forth. The gifts are in themselves gifts of great price, like those other gifts contributed by the primitive and serious Dorian tribes, their rivals. Man has to advance, we have seen, along several lines, and he does well to advance along them. 'In the morning sow thy seed, and in the evening withhold not thine hand; for thou knowest not whether shall prosper, either this or that, or whether they both shall be alike good.'

And at this moment Thucydides, a man in whom the old virtue and the new reason were in just balance, has put into the mouth of Pericles, another man of the same kind, an encomium on the modern spirit, as we may call it, of which Athens was the representative. By the mouth of Pericles, Thucydides condemned old-fashioned narrowness and illiberality. He applauded enjoyment of life. He applauded freedom from restraint. He applauded clear and fearless thinking,—the resolute bringing of our actions to the rule of reason. His expressions on this point greatly remind me of the fine saying of one of your own worthies, 'the ever-memorable Mr. John Hales, of Eton College.' 'I comprise it all,' says Hales, 'in two words: *what* and *wherefore*. That part of your burden which contains *what*, you willingly take up. But that other, which comprehends *why*, that is either too hot or too heavy; you dare not meddle with it. But I must add that also to your burden, or else I must leave you for idle persons; for without the knowledge of *why*, of the grounds or reasons of things, there is no possibility of not being deceived.' It seems to me not improbable that Hales had here in his mind the very words of the Funeral Oration: 'We do not esteem discussion a hurt to action; what we consider mischievous is rather the setting oneself to work without first getting the guidance of reason.' Finally, Thucydides applauded the quality of nature which above all others made the Athenians the men for the new era, and he used the word *eutrapelos* in its proper and natural sense, to denote the quality of happy and gracious flexibility.

Somewhat narrowed, so as to mean especially flexibility and adroitness in light social intercourse, but still employed in its natural and favourable sense, the word descends, as we saw, to Plato and Aristotle. Isocrates speaks of the quality as one which the old school regarded with alarm and disapproval; but, nevertheless, for him too the word has evidently, in itself, just the same natural and favourable sense which it has for Aristotle and Plato.

I quoted, just now, some words from the Book of Ecclesiastes, one of the wisest and one of the worst understood books in the Bible. Let us hear how the writer goes on after the words which I quoted. He proceeds thus: 'Truly the light is sweet, and a pleasant thing it is for the eyes to behold the sun; yea, if a man live many years, let him rejoice in them all; and let him remember the days of darkness, for they shall be many. All that is future is vanity. Rejoice, O young man, in thy youth, and let thy heart cheer thee in the days of thy youth, and walk in the ways of thine heart and in the sight of thine eyes;—but know thou that for all these things God will bring thee into judgment.' Let us apply these admirable words to the life and work of the Athenian people.

The old rigid order, in Greece, breaks down; a new power appears on the scene. It is the Athenian genius, with its freedom from restraint, its flexibility, its bold reason, its keen enjoyment of life. Well, let it try what it can do. Up to a certain point it is clearly in the right; possibly it may be in the right altogether. Let it have free play, and show what it can do. 'In the morning sow thy seed, and in the evening withhold not thine hand; for thou knowest not whether shall prosper, either this or that, or whether they both shall be alike good.' Whether the old line is good, or the new line, or whether they are both of them good, and must both of them be used, cannot be known without trying. Let the Athenians try, therefore, and let their genius have full swing. 'Rejoice; walk in the ways of thine heart and in the sight of thine eyes;—*but know thou that for all these things God will bring thee into judgment.*' In other words: Your enjoyment of life, your freedom from restraint, your clear and bold reason, your flexibility, are natural and excellent; but on condition that you know how to live with them, that you make a real success of them.

And a man like Pericles or Phidias seemed to afford promise that Athens would know how to make a real success of her qualities, and that an alliance between the old morality and the new freedom might be, through the admirable Athenian genius, happily established. And with such promise before his eyes, a serious man like Thucydides might well give, to the new freedom, the high and warm praise which we see given to it in the Funeral Oration.

But it soon became evident that the balance between the old morality and the new freedom was not to be maintained, and that the Athenians had the defects, as the saying is, of their qualities. Their minds were full of other things than those ideas of moral order and of right on which primitive Hellas had formed itself, and of which they themselves had, as worshippers in the shadow of the Parnassian sanctuary, once deeply felt the power. These ideas lost their predominance. The predominance for Athens,—and, indeed, for Hellas at large,—of a national religion of righteousness, of grave ideas of conduct and moral order, predominating over all other ideas, disappeared with the decline of Delphi, never to return. Not only did these ideas lose exclusive predominance, they lost all due weight. Still, indeed, they inspired poetry; and then, after inspiring the great Attic poets, Æschylus and

Sophocles, they inspired the great Attic philosophers, Socrates and Plato. But the Attic nation, which henceforth stood, in fact, for the Hellenic people, could not manage to keep its mind bent sufficiently upon them. The Attic nation had its mind bent on other things. It threw itself ardently upon other lines, which man, indeed, has to follow, which at one time, in Greece, had not been enough followed, of which Athens strongly felt the attraction, and on which it had rare gifts for excelling. The Attic nation gave its heart to those powers which we have designated, for the sake of brevity and convenience, as those of expansion, intellect, beauty, social life and manners. Athens and Greece allowed themselves to be diverted and distracted from attention to conduct, and to the ideas which inspire conduct.

It was not that the old religious beliefs of Greece, to which the ideas that inspire conduct had attached themselves, did not require to be transformed by the new spirit. They did. The greatest and best Hellenic souls, Anaxagoras, Pericles, Phidias, Sophocles, Socrates, Plato, felt, and rightly felt, that they did. The judicious historian of Greece, whom I have already quoted, Professor Curtius, says expressly: 'The popular faith was everywhere shaken, and a life resting simply on the traditionary notions was no longer possible. A dangerous rupture was at hand, unless the ancient faith were purged and elevated in such a manner as to meet the wants of the age. Mediators in this sense appeared in the persons of the great poets of Athens.' Yes, they appeared; but the current was setting too strongly another way. Poetry itself, after the death of Sophocles, 'was seized,' says Professor Curtius, 'by the same current which dissolved the foundations of the people's life, and which swept away the soil wherein the emotions of the classical period had been rooted. The old perished; but the modern age, with all its readiness in thought and speech, was incapable of creating a new art as a support to its children.'

Socrates was so penetrated with the new intellectual spirit that he was called a sophist. But the great effort of Socrates was to recover that firm foundation for human life, which a misuse of the new intellectual spirit was rendering impossible. He effected much more for after times, and for the world, than for his own people. His amount of success with Alcibiades may probably be taken as giving us, well enough, the measure of his success with the Athenian people at large. 'As to the susceptibility of Alcibiades,' we are told, 'Socrates had not come too late, for he still found in him a youthful soul, susceptible of high inspirations. But to effect in him a permanent reaction, and a lasting and fixed change of mind, was beyond the power even of a Socrates.' Alcibiades oscillated and fell away; and the Athenian people, too, and Hellas as a whole, oscillated and fell away.

So it came to pass, that after Æschylus had sadly raised his voice to deprecate 'unblessed freedom from restraint,' and after complaints had been heard, again and again, of the loss of 'the ancient morality and piety,' of 'the old elements of Hellas, reflexion and moderation, discipline and social morality,' it came to pass that finally, at the end of the Peloponnesian war, 'one result,' the historian tells us, 'one result alone admitted of no doubt; and that was, the horribly rapid progress of the demoralisation of the Hellenic nation.'

Years and centuries rolled on, and, first, the Hellenic genius issued forth invading and vanquishing with Alexander; and then, when Rome had afterwards conquered Greece, conquered the conquerors, and overspread the civilised world. And still, joined to all the gifts and graces which that admirable genius brought with it, there went, as a kind of fatal accompaniment, moral inadequacy. And if one asked why this was so, it seemed as if it could only be because the power of seriousness, of tenacious grasp upon grave and moral ideas, was wanting. And this again seemed as if it could only have for its cause, that these Hellenic natures were, in respect of their impressionability, mobility, flexibility, under the spell of a graceful but dangerous fairy, who would not let it be otherwise. 'Lest thou shouldst ponder the path of life,' says the Wise Man, '*her ways are moveable, that thou canst not know them.*' Then the new and reforming spirit, the Christain spirit, which was rising in the world, turned sternly upon this gracious flexibility, changed the sense of its name, branded it with infamy, and classed it, along with 'filthiness and foolish talking,' among 'things which are not convenient.'

Now, there you see the historical course of our words *eutrapelos, eutrapelia*, and a specimen of the range, backwards and forwards, which a single phrase in one of our Greek or Latin classics may have.

And I might go yet further, and might show you, in the mediæval world, *eutrapelia*, or flexibility, quite banished, clear straightforward Attic thinking quite lost; restraint, stoppage, and prejudice, regnant. And coming down to our own times, I might show you fearless thinking and flexibility once more, after many vicissitudes, coming into honour; and again, perhaps, not without their accompaniment of danger. And the moral from all this,—apart from the particular moral that in our classical studies we may everywhere find clues which will lead us a long way,—the moral is, not that flexibility is a bad thing, but that the Greek flexibility was really not flexible enough, because it could not enough bend itself to the moral ideas which are so large a part of life. Here, I say, is the true moral : that man has to make progress along diverse lines, in obedience to a diversity of aspirations and powers, the sum of which is truly his nature; and that he fails and falls short until he learns to advance upon them all, and to advance upon them harmoniously.

Yes, this is the moral, and we all need it, and no nation more than ours. We so easily think that life is all on one line ! Our nation, for instance, is above all things a political nation, and is apt to make far too much of politics. Many of us,—though not so very many, I suppose, of you here,—are Liberals, and think that to be a Liberal is quite enough for a man. Probably most of you here will have no difficulty in believing that to be a Liberal is not alone enough for a man, is not saving. One might even take,—and with your notions it would probably be a great treat for you,—one might take the last century of Athens, the century preceding the 'dishonest victory' of the Macedonian power, and show you a society dying of the triumph of the Liberal party. And then, again, as the young are generous, you might like to give the discomfited Liberals a respite, to let the other side have its turn; and you might consent to be shown, as you could be shown in the age of Trajan and of the Antonines, a society dying of the triumph of the Conservative party. They were excellent people, the Conservative Roman aristocracy of that epoch;—excellent, most respectable people, like the Conservatives of our own acquaintance. Only Conservatism, like Liberalism, taken alone, is not sufficient, is not of itself saving.

But you have had enough for one evening. And besides, the tendencies of the present day in education being what they are, before you proceed to hear more of this sort of thing, you ought certainly to be favoured, for several months to come, with a great many scientific lectures, and to busy yourselves considerably with the diameter of the sun and moon.

THE FRENCH PLAY IN LONDON.

ENGLISH opinion concerning France, our neighbour and rival, was formerly full of hostile prejudice, and is still, in general, quite sufficiently disposed to severity. But, from time to time, France or things French become for the solid English public the object of what our neighbours call an *enjouement*,—an infatuated interest. Such an *enjouement* Wordsworth witnessed in 1802, after the Peace of Amiens, and it disturbed his philosophic mind greatly. Every one was rushing to Paris; every one was in admiration of the First Consul:—

> Lords, lawyers, statesmen, squires of low degree,
> Men known and men unknown, sick, lame, and blind,
> Post forward all like creatures of one kind,
> With first-fruit offerings crowd to bend the knee,
> In France, before the new-born majesty.

All measure, all dignity, all real intelligence of the situation, so Wordsworth complained, were lost under the charm of the new attraction :—

'Tis ever thus. Ye men of prostrate mind,
A seemly reverence may be paid to power;
But that's a loyal virtue, never sown
In haste, nor springing with a transient shower.
When truth, when sense, when liberty were flown,
What hardship had it been to wait an hour?
Shame on you, feeble heads, to slavery prone!

One or two moralists there may still be found, who comment in a like spirit of impatience upon the extraordinary attraction exercised by the French company of actors which has lately left us. The rush of 'lords, lawyers, statesmen, squires of low degree, men known and men unknown,' of those acquainted with the French language perfectly, of those acquainted with it a little, and of those not acquainted with it at all, to the performances at the Gaiety Theatre,—the universal occupation with the performances and performers, the length and solemnity with which the newspapers chronicled and discussed them, the seriousness with which the whole repertory of the company was taken, the passion for certain pieces and for certain actors, the great ladies who by the acting of Mdlle. Sarah Bernhardt were revealed to themselves, and who could not resist the desire of telling her so,—all this has moved, I say, a surviving and aged moralist here and there amongst us to exclaim: 'Shame on you, feeble heads, to slavery prone!' The English public, according to these cynics, have been exhibiting themselves as men of prostrate mind, who pay to power a reverence anything but seemly; we have been conducting ourselves with just that absence of tact, measure, and correct perception, with all that slowness to see when one is making oneself ridiculous, which belongs to the people of our English race.

The nice sense of measure is certainly not one of Nature's gifts to her English children. But then we all of us fail in it, we natives of Great Britain; we have all of us yielded to infatuation at some moment of our lives; we are all in the same boat, and one of us has no right to laugh at the other. I am sure I have not. I remember how in my youth, after a first sight of the divine Rachel at the Edinburgh Theatre, in the part of Hermione, I followed her to Paris, and for two months never missed one of her representations. I, at least, will not cast a stone at the London public for running eagerly after the charming company of actors which has just left us; or at the great ladies who are seeking for soul and have found it in Mdlle. Sarah Bernhardt. I will not quarrel with our newspapers for their unremitting attention to these French performances, their copious criticism of them; particularly when the criticism is so interesting and so good as that which the *Times* and the *Daily News* and the *Pall Mall Gazette* have given us. Copious, indeed! —why should not our newspapers be copious on the French play, when they are copious on the Clewer case, and the Mackonochie case, and so many other matters besides, a great deal less important and interesting, all of them, than the *Maison de Molière*?

So I am not going to join the cynics, and to find fault with the *enjouement*, the infatuation, shown by the English public in its passion for the French plays and players. A passion of this kind may be salutary, if we will learn the lessons for us with which it is charged. Unfortunately, few people who feel a passion think of learning anything from it. A man feels a passion, he passes through it, and then he goes his way and straightway forgets, as the Apostle says, what manner of man he was. Above all, this is apt to happen with us English, who have, as an eminent German professor is good enough to tell us, 'so much genius, so little method.' The much genius hurries us into infatuations; the little method prevents our learning the right and wholesome lesson from them. Let us join, then, devoutly and with contrition, in the prayer of the German professor's great countryman, Goethe, a prayer which is more needful, one may surely say, for us than for him : 'God help us, and enlighten us for the time to come ! that we may not stand in our own way so much, but may have clear notions of the consequences of things!'

To get a clear notion of the consequences which do in reason follow from what we have been seeing and admiring at the Gaiety Theatre, to get a clear notion of them, and frankly to draw them, is the object which I propose to myself here. I am not going to criticise one by one the French actors and actresses who have been giving us so much pleasure. For a foreigner this must always be a task, as it seems to me, of some peril. Perilous or not, it has been abundantly attempted; and to attempt it yet again, now that the performances are over and the performers gone back to Paris, would be neither timely nor interesting. One remark I will make, a remark suggested by the inevitable comparison of Mdlle. Sarah Bernhardt with Rachel. One talks vaguely of genius, but I had never till now comprehended how much of Rachel's superiority was purely in intellectual power, how eminently this power counts in the actor's art as in all art, how just is the instinct which led the Greeks to mark with a high and severe stamp the Muses. Temperament and quick intelligence, passion, nervous mobility, grace, smile, voice, charm, poetry,—Mdlle. Sarah Bernhardt has them all. One watches her with pleasure, with admiration,—and yet not without a secret disquietude.

Something is wanting, or, at least, not present in sufficient force; something which alone can secure and fix her administration of all the charming gifts which she has, can alone keep them fresh, keep them sincere, save them from perils by caprice, perils by mannerism. That something is high intellectual power. It was here that Rachel was so great; she began, one says to oneself as one recalls her image and dwells upon it,—she began almost where Mdlle. Sarah Bernhardt ends.

But I return to my object,—the lessons to be learnt by us from the immense attraction which the French company has exercised, the consequences to be drawn from it. Certainly we have something to learn from it, and something to unlearn. What have we to unlearn? Are we to unlearn our old estimate of serious French poetry and drama? For every lover of poetry and of the drama, this is a very interesting question. In the great and serious kinds of poetry, we used to think that the French genius, admirable as in so many other ways it is, showed radical weakness. But there is a new generation growing up amongst us,—and to this young and stirring generation who of us would not gladly belong, even at the price of having to catch some of its illusions and to pass through them?—a new generation which takes French poetry and drama as seriously as Greek, and for which M.

Victor Hugo is a great poet of the race and lineage of Shakespeare.

M. Victor Hugo is a great romance-writer. There are people who are disposed to class all imaginative producers together, and to call them all by the name of poet. Then a great romance-writer will be a great poet. Above all are the French inclined to give this wide extension to the name poet, and the inclination is very characteristic of them. It betrays that very defect which we have mentioned, the inadequacy of their genius in the higher regions of poetry. If they were more at home in those regions, they would feel the essential difference between imaginative production in verse, and imaginative production in prose, too strongly, to be ever inclined to call both by the common name of poetry. They would perceive with us, that M. Victor Hugo, for instance, or Sir Walter Scott, may be a great romance-writer, and may yet be by no means a great poet.

Poetry is simply the most delightful and perfect form of utterance that human words can reach. Its rhythm and measure, elevated to a regularity, certainty, and force very different from that of the rhythm and measure which can pervade prose, are a part of its perfection. The more of genius that a nation has for high poetry, the more will the rhythm and measure which its poetical utterance adopts be distinguished by adequacy and beauty. That is why M. Henry Cochin's remark on Shakespeare, which I have elsewhere quoted, is so good : 'Shakespeare is not only,' says M. Henry Cochin, 'the king of the realm of thought, he is also the king of poetic rhythm and style. Shakespeare has succeeded in giving us the most varied, the most harmonious verse, which has ever sounded upon the human ear since the verse of the Greeks.'

Let us have a line or two of Shakespeare's verse before us, just to supply the mind with a standard of reverence in the discussion of this matter. We may take the lines from him almost at random :—

> Five hundred poor I have in yearly pay,
> Who twice a day their wither'd hands hold up
> Toward heaven, to pardon blood ; and I have built
> Two chantries, where the sad and solemn priests
> Sing still for Richard's soul.

Yes, there indeed is the verse of Shakespeare, the verse of the highest English poetry ; there is what M. Henry Cochin calls 'the majestic English iambic !' We will not inflict Greek upon our readers, but every one who knows Greek will remember that the iambic of the Attic tragedians is a rhythm of the same high and splendid quality.

Which of us doubts that imaginative production, uttering itself in such a form as this, is altogether another and a higher thing from imaginative production uttering itself in any of the forms of prose? And if we find a nation doubting whether there is any great difference between imaginative and eloquent production in verse and imaginative and eloquent production in prose, and inclined to call all imaginative producers by the common name of poets, then we may be sure of one thing : namely, that this nation has never yet succeeded in finding the highest and most adequate form for poetry. Because, if it had, it could never have doubted of the essential superiority of this form to all prose forms of utterance. And if a nation has never succeeded in creating this high and adequate form for its poetry, then we may conclude that it is not gifted with the genius for high poetry ; since the genius for high poetry calls forth the high and adequate form, and is inseparable from it. So that, on the one hand, from the absence of conspicuous genius in a people for poetry, we may predict the absence of an adequate poetical form ; and on the other hand, again, from the want of an adequate poetical form, we may infer the want of conspicuous national genius for poetry.

And we may proceed, supposing that our estimate of a nation's success in poetry is said to be much too low, and is called in question, in either of two ways. If we are said to underrate, for instance, the production of Corneille and Racine in poetry, we may compare this production in power, in penetrativeness, in criticism of life, in ability to call forth our energy and joy, with the production of Homer and Shakespeare. M. Victor Hugo is said to be a poet of the race and lineage of Shakespeare, and I hear astonishment expressed at my not ranking him much above Wordsworth. Well, then, compare their production, in cases where it lends itself to a comparison. Compare the poetry of the moonlight scene in *Hernani*, really the most poetical scene in that play, with the poetry of the moonlight scene in the *Merchant of Venice*. Compare

> . . . Sur nous, tout en dormant,
> La nature à demi veille amoureusement—

with

> Sit, Jessica; look how the floor of heaven
> Is thick inlaid with patines of bright gold!

Compare the laudation of their own country, an inspiring but also a trying theme for a poet, by Shakespeare and Wordsworth on the one hand, and by M. Victor Hugo on the other. Compare Shakespeare's '

> This precious stone set in the silver sea,
> This blessed plot, this earth, this realm, this England—

or compare Wordsworth's

> We must be free or die, who speak the tongue
> Which Shakespeare spake, the faith and morals hold
> Which Milton held . . . .

with M. Victor Hugo's

> Non, France, l'univers a besoin que tu vives!
> Je le redis, la France est un besoin des hommes.

Who does not recognise the difference of spirit here? And the difference is, that the English lines have the distinctive spirit of high poetry, and the French lines have not.

Here we have been seeking to attend chiefly to the contents and spirit of the verses chosen. Let us now attend, so far as we can, to form only, and the result will be the same. We will confine ourselves, since our subject is the French play in London, to dramatic verse. We require an adequate form of verse for high poetic drama. The acepted form with the French is the rhymed Alexandrine. Let us keep the iambic of the Greeks or of Shakespeare, let us keep such verse as,

> This precious stone set in a silver sea,

present to our minds. Then let us take such verse as this from *Hernani*:—

> Le comte d'Onate, qui l'aime aussi, la garde
> Et comme un majordome et comme un amoureux.
> Quelque reître, une nuit, *gardien peu langoureux*,
> Pourrait bien, &c. &c.

or as this, from the same:—

> Quant à lutter ensemble
> Sur le terrain d'amour, *beau champ qui toujours tremble*,
> De fadaises, mon cher, je sais mal faire assaut.

The words in italics will suffice to give us, I think, the sense of what constitutes the fatal fault of the rhyming Alexandrine of French tragedy,—its incurable artificiality, its want of the fluidity, the naturalness, the rapid forward movement of true dramatic verse. M. Victor Hugo is said to be a cunning and mighty artist in Alexandrines, and so unquestionably he is; but he is an artist in a form radically inadequate and inferior, and in which a drama like that of Sophocles or Shakespeare is impossible.

It happens that in our own language we have an example of the employment of an inadequate form in tragedy and in elevated poetry, and can see the result of it. The rhymed ten-syllable couplet, the heroic couplet as it is often called, is such a form. In the earlier work of Shakespeare, work adopted or adapted by him even if not altogether his own work, we find this form often employed:—

> Alas! what joy shall noble Talbot have
> To bid his young son welcome to his grave?
> Away! vexation almost stops my breath
> That sundered friends greet in the hour of death.
> Lucy, farewell; no more my future can
> But curse the cause I cannot aid the man.

Maine, Blois, Poitiers and Tours are won away
'Long all of Somerset and his delay.

Traces of this form remain in Shakespeare's work to the last, in the rhyming of final couplets. But because he had so great a genius for true tragic poetry, Shakespeare dropped this necessarily inadequate form and took a better. We find the rhymed couplet again in Dryden's tragedies. But this vigorous rhetorical poet had no real genius for true tragic poetry, and his form is itself a proof of it. True tragic poetry is impossible with this inadequate form. Again, all through the eighteenth century this form was dominant as the main form for high efforts in English poetry; and our serious poetry of that century, accordingly, has something inevitably defective and unsatisfactory. When it rises out of this, it at the same time adopts instinctively a truer form, as Gray does in the *Elegy*. The just and perfect use of the ten-syllable couplet is to be seen in Chaucer. As a form for tragedy, and for poetry of the most serious and elevated kind, it is defective. It makes real adequacy in poetry of this kind impossible; and its prevalence, for poetry of this kind, proves that those amongst whom it prevails have for poetry of this kind no signal gift.

The case of the great Molière himself will illustrate the truth of what I say. Molière is by far the chief name in French poetry; he is one of the very greatest names in all literature. He has admirable and delightful power, penetrativeness, insight; a masterly criticism of life. But he is a comic poet. Why? Had he no seriousness and depth of nature? He had profound seriousness. And would not a dramatic poet with this depth of nature be a tragedian if he could? Of course he would. For only by breasting in full the storm and cloud of life, breasting it and passing through it and above it, can the dramatist who feels the weight of mortal things liberate himself from the pressure, and rise, as we all seek to rise, to content and joy. Tragedy breasts the pressure of life. Comedy eludes it, half liberates itself from it by irony. But the tragedian, if he has the sterner labour, has also the higher prize. Shakespeare has more joy than Molière, more assurance and peace. *Othello*, with all its passion and terror, is on the whole a work animating and fortifying; more so a thousand times than *George Dandin*, which is mournfully depressing. Molière, if he could, would have given us Othellos instead of George Dandins; let us not doubt it. If he did not give Othellos to us, it was because the highest sort of poetic power was wanting to him. And if the highest sort of poetic power had been not wanting to him but present, he would have found no adequate form of dramatic verse for conveying it, he would have had to create one. For such tasks Molière had not power; and this is only another way of saying that for the highest tasks in poetry the genius of his nation appears to have not power. But serious spirit and great poet that he was, Molière had far too sound an instinct to attempt so earnest a matter as tragic drama with inadequate means. It would have been a heart-breaking business for him. He did not attempt it, therefore, but confined himself to comedy.

The *Misanthrope* and the *Tartuffe* are comedy, but they are comedy in verse, poetic comedy. They employ the established verse of French dramatic poetry, the Alexandrine. Immense power has gone to the making of them; a world of vigorous sense, piercing observation, pathetic meditation, profound criticism of life. Molière had also one great advantage as a dramatist over Shakespeare; he wrote for a more developed theatre, a more developed society. Moreover he was at the same time, probably, by nature a better *theatre-poet* than Shakespeare; he had a keener sense for theatrical situation. Shakespeare is not rightly to be called, as Goethe calls him, an epitomator rather than a dramatist; but he may rightly be called rather a dramatist than a theatre-poet. Molière, —and here his French nature stood him in good stead,— was a theatre-poet of the very first order. Comedy, too, escapes, as has been already said, the test of entire seriousness; it remains, by the law of its being, in a region of comparative lightness and of irony. What is artificial can pass in comedy more easily. In spite of all these advantages, the *Misanthrope* and the *Tartuffe* have, and have by reason of their poetic form, an artificiality which makes itself too much felt, and which provokes weariness. The freshness and power of Molière are best felt when he uses prose, in pieces such as the *Avare*, or the *Fourberies de Scapin*, or *George Dandin*. How entirely the contrary is the case with Shakespeare; how undoubtedly is it his verse which shows his power most! But so inadequate a vehicle for dramatic poetry is the French Alexandrine, that its sway hindered Molière, one may think, from being a tragic poet at all, in spite of his having gifts for this highest form of dramatic poetry which are immeasurably superior to those of any other French poet. And in comedy, where Molière thought he could use the Alexandrine, and where he did use it with splendid power, it yet in a considerable degree hampered and lamed him, so that this true and great poet is actually most satisfactory in his prose.

If Molière cannot make us insensible to the inherent defects of French dramatic poetry, still less can Corneille and Racine. Corneille has energy and nobility, Racine an often Virgilian sweetness and pathos. But while Molière in depth, penetrativeness, and powerful criticism of life, belongs to the same family as Sophocles and Shakespeare, Corneille and Racine are quite of another order. We must not be misled by the excessive estimate of them among their own countrymen. I remember an answer of M. Sainte-Beuve, who always treated me with great kindness, and to whom I once ventured to say that I could not think Lamartine a poet of very high importance. 'He was important to *us*,' answered M. Sainte-Beuve. In a far higher degree can a Frenchman say of Corneille and Racine: 'They were important to *us*.' Voltaire pronounces of them: 'These men taught our nation to think, to feel, and to express itself.' *Ces hommes enseignèrent à la nation à penser, à sentir et à s'exprimer.* They were thus the instructors and formers of a society in many respects the most civilised and consummate that the world has ever seen, and which certainly has not been inclined to underrate its own advantages. How natural, then, that it should feel grateful to its formers, and should extol them! 'Tell your brother Rodolphe,' writes Joseph de Maistre from Russia to his daughter at home, 'to get on with his French poets; let him have them by heart,—the inimitable Racine above all; never mind whether he understands him or not. I did not understand him, when my mother used to come and sit on my bed, and repeat from him, and put me to sleep with her beautiful voice to the sound of this incomparable music. I knew hundreds of lines of him before I could read ; and that is why my ears, having drunk in this ambrosia betimes, have never been able to endure common stuff since.' What a spell must such early use have had for riveting the affections; and how civilising are such affections, how honourable to the society which can be imbued with them, to the literature which can inspire them ! Pope was in a similar way, though not at all in the same degree, a forming and civilising influence to our grandfathers, and limited their literary taste while he stimulated and formed it. So, too, the Greek boy was fed by his mother and nurse with Homer ; but then in this case it was Homer !

We English had Shakespeare waiting to open our eyes, whensoever a favourable moment came, to the insufficiencies of Pope. But the French had no Shakespeare to open their eyes to the insufficiencies of Corneille and Racine. Great artists like Talma and Rachel, whose power, as actors, was far superior to the power, as poets, of the dramatists whose work they were rendering, filled out with their own life and warmth the parts into which they threw themselves, gave body to what was meagre, fire to what was cold, and themselves supported the poetry of the French classic drama rather than were supported by it. It was easier to think the poetry of Racine inimitable, when Talma or Rachel were seen producing in it such inimitable effects. Indeed French acting is so good, that there are few pieces, excepting always those of Molière, in the repertory of a company such as that which we have just seen, where the actors do not show themselves to be superior to the pieces they render, and to be worthy of pieces which are better. *Phèdre* is a work of much beauty, yet certainly one felt this in seeing Rachel in the part of Phèdre. I am not sure that one feels it in seeing Mdlle. Sarah Bernhardt as Phèdre, but I am sure that one feels it in seeing her as Doña Sol.

The tragedy of M. Victor Hugo has always, indeed, stirring events in plenty; and so long as the human nerves are what they are, so long will things like the sounding of the horn, in the famous fifth act of *Hernani*, produce a thrill in us. But so will Werner's *Twenty-fourth of February*, or Scott's *House of Aspen*. A thrill of this sort may be raised in us, and yet our poetic sense may remain profoundly dissatisfied. So it remains in *Hernani*. M. Sarcey, a critic always acute and intelligent, and whom one reads with profit and pleasure, says that we English are fatigued by the long speeches in *Hernani*, and that we do not appreciate what delights French people in it, the splendour of the verse, the wondrous beauty of the style, the poetry. Here recurs the question as to the adequacy of the French Alexandrine as tragic verse. If this form is vitally inadequate for tragedy, then to speak absolutely of splendour of verse and wondrous beauty of style in it when employed for tragedy, is misleading. Beyond doubt M. Victor Hugo has an admirable gift for versification. So had Pope. But to speak absolutely of the splendour of verse and wondrous beauty of style of the *Essay on Man* would be misleading. Such terms can be properly used only of verse and style of an altogether higher and more adequate kind, a verse and style like that of Dante, Shakespeare, or Milton. Pope's brilliant gift for versification is exercised within the limits of a form inadequate for true philosophic poetry, and by its very presence excluding it. M. Victor Hugo's brilliant gift for versification is exercised within the limits of a form inadequate for true tragic poetry, and by its very presence excluding it.

But, if we are called upon to prove this from the poetry itself, instead of inferring it from the form, our task, in the case of *Hernani*, is really only too easy. What is the poetical value of this famous fifth act of *Hernani*? What poetical truth, or verisimilitude, or possibility has Ruy Gomez, this chivalrous old Spanish grandee, this venerable nobleman, who, because he cannot marry his niece, presents himself to her and her husband upon their wedding night, and insists on the husband performing an old promise to commit suicide if summoned by Ruy Gomez to do so? Naturally the poor young couple raise difficulties, and the venerable nobleman keeps plying them with: *Bois! Allons! Le sépulcre est ouvert, et je ne puis attendre! J'ai hâte! Il faut mourir!* This is a mere character of Surrey melodrama. And Hernani, who, when he is reminded that it is by his father's head that he has sworn to commit suicide, exclaims:

Mon père! mon père!—Ah! j'en perdrai la raison!

and who, when Doña Sol gets the poison away from him, entreats her to return it:—

Par pitié, ce poison,
Rends-le-moi! Par l'amour, par notre âme immortelle!

because

Le duc a ma parole, et mon père est là-haut!

The *poetry*! says M. Sarcey;—and one thinks of the poetry of *Lear*! M. Sarcey must pardon me for saying, that in

Le duc a ma parole, et mon père est là-haut!

we are not in the world of poetry at all, hardly even in the world of literature, unless it be the literature of *Bombastes Furioso*.

Our sense, then, for what is poetry and what is not, the attractiveness of the French plays and players must not make us unlearn. We may and must retain our old conviction of the fundamental insufficiency, both in substance and in form, of the rhymed tragedy of the French. We are to keep, too, what in the main has always been the English estimate of Molière : that he is a man of creative and splendid power, a dramatist whose work is truly delightful, is edifying and immortal; but that even Molière, in poetic drama, is hampered and has not full swing, and, in consequence, leaves us somewhat dissatisfied. Finally, we poor old people should pluck up courage to stand out yet, for the few years of life which yet remain to us, against that passing illusion of the confident young generation who are newly come out on the war-path, that M. Victor Hugo is a poet of the race and lineage of Shakespeare.

What, now, are we to say of the prose drama of modern life, the drama of which the *Sphinx* and the *Etrangère* and the *Demi-Monde* are types, and which was the most strongly attractive part, probably, of the feast offered to us by the French company? The first thing to be said of these pieces is that they are admirably acted. But then constantly, as I have already said, one has the feeling that the French actors are better than the pieces which they play. What are we to think of this modern prose drama in itself, the drama of M. Octave Feuillet, and M. Alexandre Dumas the younger, and M. Augier? Some of the pieces composing it are better constructed and written than others, and much more effective. But this whole drama has one character common to it all. It may be best described as the theatre of the *homme sensuel moyen*, the average sensual man, whose country is France, and whose city is Paris, and whose ideal is the free, gay, pleasurable life of Paris,—an ideal which our young literary generation, now out on the war-path here in England, seek to adopt from France, and which they busily preach and work for. Of course there is in Paris much life of another sort too, as there are in France many men of another type than that of the *homme sensuel moyen*. But for many reasons, which I need not enumerate here, the life of the free, confident, harmonious development of the senses, all round, has been able to establish itself among the French, and at Paris, as it has established itself nowhere else; and the ideal life of Paris is this sort of life triumphant. And of this ideal the modern French drama, works like the *Sphinx* and the *Etrangère* and the *Demi-Monde*, are the expression. It is the drama, I say, this drama now in question, of the *homme sensuel moyen*, the average sensual man. It represents the life of the senses developing themselves all round without misgiving; a life confident, fair and free, with fireworks of fine emotions, grand passions and devotedness,—or rather, perhaps, we should say *dévouement*,—lighting it up when necessary.

We in England have no modern drama at all. We have our Elizabethan drama. We have a drama of the last century and of the latter part of the century preceding, a drama which may be called our drama of *the town*, when *the town* was an entity powerful enough, because homogeneous enough, to evoke a drama embodying its notions of life. But we have no modern drama. Our vast society is not at present homogeneous enough for this,— not sufficiently united, even any large portion of it, in a common view of life, a common ideal, capable of serving as basis for a modern English drama. We have apparitions of poetic and romantic drama (as the French, too, have their charming *Gringoire*), which are always possible, because man has always in his nature the poetical fibre. Then we have numberless imitations and adaptations from the French. All of these are at the bottom fantastic. We may truly say of them, that 'truth and sense and liberty are flown.' And the reason is evident. They are pages out of a life which the ideal of the *homme sensuel moyen* rules, transferred to a life where this ideal, notwithstanding the fervid adhesion to it of our young generation, does not reign. For the attentive observer the result is a sense of incurable falsity in the piece as adapted. Let me give an example. Everybody remembers *Pink Dominoes*. The piece turns upon an incident possible and natural enough in the life of Paris. Transferred to the life of London the incident is altogether unreal, and its unreality makes the whole piece, in its English form, fantastic and absurd.

Still that does not prevent such pieces, and the theatre generally, from now exercising upon us a great attraction. For we are at the end of a period, and have to deal with the facts and symptoms of a new period on which we are entering; and prominent among these fresh facts and symptoms is the irresistibility of the theatre. We know how the Elizabethan theatre had its cause in an ardent zest for life and living, a bold and large curiosity, a desire for a fuller, richer existence, pervading this nation at large, as they pervaded other nations, after the long mediæval time of obstruction and restraint. But we know, too, how the great middle class of this nation, alarmed at grave symptoms which showed themselves in the new movement, drew back; made choice for its spirit to live at one point, instead of living, or trying to live, at many; entered, as I have so often said, the prison of Puritanism, and had the key turned upon its spirit there for two hundred years. Our middle class forsook the theatre. The English theatre reflected no more the aspiration of a great community for a fuller and richer sense of human existence.

This theatre came afterwards, however, to reflect the aspirations of 'the town.' It developed a drama to suit these aspirations; while it also brought back and re-exhibited the Elizabethan drama, so far as 'the town' wanted it and liked it. Finally, as even 'the town' ceased to be homogeneous, the theatre ceased to develope anything expressive. It still repeated what was old with more or less of talent. But the mass of our English community, the mass of the middle class, kept aloof from the whole thing.

I remember how, happening to be at Shrewsbury, twenty years ago, and finding the whole Haymarket company acting there, I went to the theatre. Never was there such a scene of desolation. Scattered at very distant intervals through the boxes were about half-a-dozen chance-comers like myself; there were some soldiers and their friends in the pit, and a good many riff-raff in the upper gallery. The real townspeople, the people who carried forward the business and life of Shrewsbury, and who filled its churches and chapels on Sundays, were entirely absent. I pitied the excellent Haymarket company; it must have been like acting to oneself upon an iceberg. Here one had a good example,—as I thought at the time, and as I have often thought since,—of the complete estrangement of the British middle class from the theatre.

What is certain is, that a signal change is coming over us, and that it has already made great progress. It is said that there are now forty theatres in London. Even in Edinburgh, where in old times a single theatre maintained itself under protest, there are now, I believe, over half-a-dozen. The change is not due only to an increased liking in the upper class and in the working class for the theatre. Their liking for it has certainly increased, but this is not enough to account for the change. The attraction of the theatre begins to be felt again, after a long interval of insensibility, by the middle class also. Our French friends would say that this class, long petrified in a narrow Protestantism and in a perpetual reading of the Bible, is beginning at last to grow conscious of the horrible unnaturalness and *ennui* of its life, and is seeking to escape from it. Undoubtedly the type of religion to which the British middle class has sacrificed the theatre, as it has sacrificed so much besides, is defective. But I prefer to say that this great class, having had the discipline of its religion, is now awakening to the sure truth that the human spirit cannot live aright if it lives at one point only, that it can and ought to live at several points at the same time. The human spirit has a vital need, as we say, for conduct and religion ; but it has the need also for expansion, for intellect and knowledge, for beauty, for social life and manners. The revelation of these additional needs brings the middle class to the theatre.

The revelation was indispensable, the needs are real, the theatre is one of the mightiest means of satisfying them, and the theatre, therefore, is irresistible. That conclusion, at any rate, we may take for certain. We have to unlearn, therefore, our long disregard of the theatre; we have to own that the theatre is irresistible.

But I see our community turning to the theatre with eagerness, and finding the English theatre without organisation, or purpose, or dignity, and no modern English drama at all except a fantastical one. And then I see the French company from the chief theatre of Paris showing themselves to us in London,—a society of actors admirable in organisation, purpose, and dignity, with a modern drama not fantastic at all, but corresponding with fidelity to a very palpable and powerful ideal, the ideal of the life of the *homme sensuel moyen* in Paris, his beautiful city. I see in England a materialised upper class, sensible of the nullity of our own modern drama, impatient of the state of false constraint and of blank to which the Puritanism of our middle class has brought our stage and much of our life, delighting in such drama as the modern drama of Paris. I see the emancipated youth of both sexes delighting in it ; the new and clever newspapers, which push on the work of emancipation and serve as devoted missionaries of the gospel of the life of Paris and of the ideal of the average sensual man, delighting in it. And in this condition of affairs I see the middle class beginning to arrive at the theatre again after an abstention of two centuries and more ; arriving eager and curious, but a little bewildered.

Now, lest at this critical moment such drama as the *Sphinx* and the *Etrangère* and the *Demi-Monde,* positive as it is, and powerful as it is, and pushed as it is, and played with such prodigious care and talent, should too much rule the situation, let us take heart of grace and say, that as the right conclusion from the unparalleled success of the French company was not that we should reverse our old notions about the tragedy of M. Victor Hugo, or about French classic tragedy, or even about the poetic drama of the great Molière, so neither is it the right conclusion from this success that we should be converted and become believers in the legitimacy of the life-ideal of the *homme sensuel moyen,* and in the sufficiency of his drama. This is not the occasion to deliver a moral discourse. It is enough to revert to what has been already said, and to remark that the French ideal and its theatre have the defect of leaving out too much of life, of treating the soul as if it lived at one point or group of points only, of ignoring other points, or groups of points, at which it must live as well. And herein the conception of life shown in this French ideal and in its drama really resembles, different as in other ways they are, the conception of life prevalent with the British middle class, and has the like kind of defect. Both conceptions of life are too narrow. Sooner or later, if we adopt either, our soul and spirit are starved, and go amiss, and suffer.

What then, finally, *are* we to learn from the marvellous success and attractiveness of the performances at the Gaiety Theatre? What *is* the consequence which it is right and rational for us to draw? Surely it is this: 'The theatre is irresistible; *organise the theatre.*' Surely, if we wish to stand less in our own way, and to have clear notions of the consequences of things, it is to this conclusion that we should come.

The performances of the French company show us plainly, I think, what is gained,—the theatre being admitted to be an irresistible need for civilised communities,—by organising the theatre. Some of the drama played by this company is, as we have seen, questionable. But, in the absence of an organisation such as that of this company, it would be played even yet more ; it would, with a still lower drama to accompany it, almost if not altogether reign ; it would have far less correction and relief by better things. An older and better drama, containing many things of high merit, some things of surpassing merit, is kept before the public by means of this company, is given frequently, is given to perfection. Pieces of truth and beauty, which emerge here and there among the questionable pieces of the modern drama, get the benefit of this company's skill, and are given to perfection. The questionable pieces themselves lose something of their unprofitableness and vice in their hands ; the acting carries us into the world of correct and pleasing art, if the piece does not. And the type of perfection fixed by these fine actors influences for good every actor in France.

Moreover, the French company shows us not only what is gained by organising the theatre, but what is meant by organising it. The organisation in the example before us is simple and rational. We have a society of good actors, with a grant from the State on condition of their giving with frequency the famous and classic stage-plays of their nation, and with a commissioner of the State attached to the society and taking part in council with it. But the society is to all intents and purposes self-governing. And in connexion with the society is the school of dramatic elocution of the *Conservatoire*, a school with the names of Regnier, Monrose, Got and Delaunay on its roll of professors.

The Society of the French Theatre dates from Louis the Fourteenth and from France's great century. It has, therefore, traditions, effect, consistency, and a place in the public esteem, which are not to be won in a day. But its organisation is such as a judicious man, desiring the results which in France have been by this time won, would naturally have devised ; and it is such as a judicious man, desiring in another country to secure like results, would naturally imitate.

We have in England everything to make us dissatisfied with the chaotic and ineffective condition into which our theatre has fallen. We have the remembrance of better things in the past, and the elements for better things in the future. We have a splendid national drama of the Elizabethan age, and a later drama of 'the town' which has no lack of pieces conspicuous by their stage-qualities, their vivacity and their talent, and interesting by their pictures of manners. We have had great actors. We have good actors not a few at the present moment. But we have been unlucky, as we so often are, in the work of organisation. In the essay at organisation which in the patent theatres, with their exclusive privilege of acting Shakespeare, we formerly had, we find by no means an example, such as we have in the constitution of the French Theatre, of what a judicious man, seeking the good of the drama and of the public, would naturally devise. We find rather such a machinery as might be devised by a man prone to stand in his own way, a man devoid of clear notions of the consequences of things. It was inevitable that the patent theatres should provoke discontent and attack. They were attacked, and their privilege fell. Still, to this essay, however imperfect, of a public organisation for the English theatre, our stage owes the days of power and greatness which it has enjoyed. So far as we have had a school of great actors, so far as our stage has had tradition, effect, consistency, and a hold on public esteem, it had them under the system of the privileged theatres. The system had its faults, and was abandoned; but then, instead of devising a better plan of public organisation for the English theatre, we gladly took refuge in our favourite doctrines of the mischief of State interference, of the blessedness of leaving every man free to do as he likes, of the impertinence of presuming to check any man's natural taste for the bathos and pressing him to relish the sublime. We left the

English theatre to take its chance. Its present impotence is the result.

It seems to me that every one of us is concerned to find a remedy for this melancholy state of things; and that the pleasure we have had in the visit of the French company is barren, unless it leaves us with the impulse to mend the condition of our theatre, and with the lesson how alone it can be rationally attempted. 'Forget,'—can we not hear these fine artists saying in an undertone to us, amidst their graceful compliments of adieu?—'forget your clap-trap, and believe that the State, the nation in its collective and corporate character, does well to concern itself about an influence so important to national life and manners as the theatre. Form a company out of the materials ready to your hand in your many good actors or actors of promise. Give them a theatre at the West End. Let them have a grant from your Science and Art Department; let some intelligent and accomplished man, like our friend Mr. Pigott, your present Examiner of Plays, be joined to them as Commissioner from the Department, to see that the conditions of the grant are observed. Let the conditions of the grant be that a repertory is agreed upon, taken out of the works of Shakespeare and out of the volumes of the *Modern British Drama*, and that pieces from this repertory are played a certain number of times in each season ; as to new pieces, let your company use its discretion. Let a school of dramatic elocution and declamation be instituted in connexion with your company. It may surprise you to hear that elocution and declamation are things to be taught and learnt, and do not come by nature ; but it is so. Your best and most serious actors' (this is added with a smile) 'would have been better, if in their youth they had learnt elocution. These recommendations, you may think, are not very much ; but, as your divine William says, they are enough ; they will serve. Try them. When your institution in the West of London has become a success, plant a second of like kind in the East. The people *will* have the theatre ; then make it a good one. Let your two or three chief provincial towns institute, with municipal subsidy and co-operation, theatres such as you institute in the metropolis with State subsidy and co-operation. So you will restore the English theatre. And then a modern drama of your own will also, probably, spring up amongst you, and you will not have to come to us for pieces like *Pink Dominoes*.'

No, and we will hope, too, that the modern English drama, when it comes, may be something different from even the *Sphinx* and the *Demi-Monde*. For my part, I have all confidence, that if it ever does come, it will be different and better. But let us not say a word to wound the feelings of those who have given us so much pleasure, and who leave to us as a parting legacy such excellent advice. For excellent advice it is, and everything we saw these artists say and do upon the Gaiety stage inculcates it for us, whether they exactly formulated it in words or no. And still, even now that they are gone, when I pass along the Strand and come opposite to the Gaiety Theatre, I see a fugitive vision of delicate features under a shower of hair and a cloud of lace, and hear the voice of Mdlle. Sarah Bernhardt saying in its most caressing tones to the Londoners : ' The theatre is irresistible ; *organise the theatre* !'

COPYRIGHT.

GEORGE SAND died in 1876, and her publisher, Michel Lévy, died the year before, in 1875. In May, 1875, just after Michel Lévy's death, Madame Sand wrote a letter in which she renders a tribute of praise and gratitude to the memory of that enterprising, sagacious, and successful man. She describes his character, his habits, his treatment of his authors, his way of doing business, his conception of the book-trade and of its prospects. It was by this conception and by the line which he boldly took in pursuance of it that he was original and remarkable; a main creator, says Madame Sand, of our new *modus vivendi* in literature; one whose disappearance is not the disappearance of a rich man merely, but of an intellectual force.

The industrial and literary revolution, for which Michel Lévy did so much, may be summed up in two words: *cheap books*. But by cheap books we are not to understand the hideous and ignoble things with which, under this name, England and America have made us familiar. Cheap books in the revolution of Michel Lévy, were books in the *format Charpentier* or the *format Lévy*, books in duodecimo instead of octavo; and costing, in general, two-and-sixpence or three shillings a volume instead of eight shillings or nine shillings. But they were still books of such an outward form and fashion as to satisfy a decent taste, not to revolt it; books shapely, well printed, well margined; agreeable to look upon and clear to read.

Such as it was, however, the cheapening of their books threw, at first, French authors into alarm. They thought that it threatened their interests. 'I remember the time, not so very long ago,' says Madame Sand, 'when we replied to the publishers who were demonstrating to us what the results of the future would be: "Yes, if you succeed, it will be all very well; but if you fail, if, after an immense issue of books, you do not diffuse the taste for reading, then you are lost, and we along with you." And I urged upon Michel Lévy,' she continues, 'this objection among others, that frivolous or unhealthy books attracted the masses, to the exclusion of works which are useful and conscientious. He replied to me with that practical intelligence which he possessed in so eminent a degree: "Possibly, and even probably, it may be so at first. But consider this: that the reading of bad books has inevitably one good result. It inspires a man with the curiosity to read, it gives him the habit of reading, and the habit becomes a necessity. I intend, that, before ten years are over, people shall ask for their book as impatiently as if it were a question of dinner when one is hungry. Food and books, we have to create a state of things when both shall alike be felt as needs; and you will confess then, you writers and artists, that we have solved your problem: *Man does not live by bread alone.*"'

The ten years were not ended before Michel Lévy's authors had to own, says Madame Sand, that their publisher was right. Madame Sand adds that this led her to reflect on the value of the mediocre in art and literature. Illustrious friends and fellow-authors of hers had been in despair at seeing works of the third order obtain a success far beyond any that they could expect for their own works, and they were disposed to think that with cheap books an era of literary decadence was opening. You are misled, she tells them, by the passing disturbance which important innovations always create at first. It was thought, when railways came, that we had seen the last of conveyance by horses and carriages, and that the providers of it must all be ruined; but it turns out that railways have created a business for horses and carriages greater than there ever was before. In the same way, the abundant consumption of middling literature has stimulated the appetite for trying to know and to judge books. Second-rate, commonplace literature is what the ignorant require for catching the first desire for books, the first gleam of light; the day will presently dawn for them as it does for the child, who by degrees, as he learns to read, learns to understand also; and, in fifty years from this time, the bad and the middling in literature will be unable to find a publisher, because they will be unable to find a market.

So prophesied George Sand, and the prophecy was certainly a bold one. May we really hope, that towards the year 1930 the bad and the middling in literature will, either in Paris or in London, be unable to find a publisher because it will be unable to find a market? Let us all do our best to bring about such a consummation, without, however, too confidently counting upon it.

But that on which I at present wish to dwell, in this relation by Madame Sand of her debate with her energetic publisher and of her own reflexions on it, is the view presented of the book-trade and of its future. That view I believe to be in the main sound, and to show the course which things do naturally and properly tend to take, in England as well as in France. I do not say that I quite adopt the theory offered by Michel Lévy, and accepted by George Sand, to explain the course which things are thus taking. I do not think it safe to say, that the consumption of the bad and middling in literature does of itself necessarily engender a taste for the good, and that out of the multiplication of second-rate books for the million the multiplication of first-rate books does as a natural consequence spring. But the facts themselves, I think, are as Michel Lévy laid them down, though one may dispute his explanation and filiation for the facts. It is a fact that there is a need for cheaper books, and that authors and publishers may comply with it and yet not be losers. It is a fact that the masses, when they first take to reading, will probably read a great deal of rubbish, and yet that the victory will be with good books in the end. In part we can see that this is the course which things are actually taking; in part we can predict, from knowing the deepest and strongest instincts which govern mankind in its development,—the instinct of expansion, the instinct of self-preservation,—that it is the course which things will take in the future.

The practical mode by which Michel Lévy revolutionised the book-trade was this. He brought out in the *format Lévy*, at three francs or three francs and a half a volume, new works such as, for example, those of George Sand herself, which formerly would have come out at seven francs and a half a volume. Nay, such works would very often have taken two volumes, costing fifteen francs, to give no more than what is given in one volume of the *format Lévy* for three francs and a half. New books in octavo were cheapened likewise. The two octavo volumes, in French, of Prince Metternich's Memoirs and Correspondence, which have lately come out in Paris, cost but eighteen francs. The two octavo volumes of the English version of Prince Metternich's Memoirs and Correspondence cost thirty-six shillings. But in general we may say that the important reform accomplished in the French book-trade by Michel Lévy and by other publishers of like mind with him was this: to give to the public, in the *format Lévy*, new books at half-a-crown or three shillings, instead of at from six to twelve shillings.

And now to apply this, where it seems to me to be of very useful application, to various points which emerge in discussing the copyright of English authors and the conditions of the English book-trade. I leave on one side all questions of copyright in acted plays, music, and pictures. I confine myself to copyright in books, and to the chief questions raised on it. My point of view will be neither an author's point of view, nor a publisher's point of view, nor yet the point of view of one contending against authors or publishers, but the point of view of one whose sole wish is to let things appear to him fairly and naturally, and as they really are.

A Royal Commission on Copyright has lately been sitting, and has made its report. 'We have arrived at a conclusion,' the report declares, 'that copyright should continue to be treated by law as a proprietary right, and that it is not expedient to substitute for this a right to a royalty, or any other of a similar kind.'

This opening sentence of the report refers to a great battle. The Commissioners have come, they say, to a conclusion that 'copyright should continue to be treated as a *proprietary right.*' Here has been the point of conflict, —as to the proprietary right of the author, as to his right of property in his production. Never perhaps do men show themselves so earnest, so pertinacious, so untiringly ingenious, as when they have under discussion the right and idea of property. One is reminded of Pascal: 'This dog is *mine,* said these poor children ; behold *my* place in the sun !' It is disputed whether an author has the right of property in his production after he has once published it. Professor Huxley and Mr. Herbert Spencer contended with indefatigable ingenuity before the Royal Commission on Copyright that he has; and Mr. Farrer, of the Board of Trade, and Sir Louis Mallet maintained resolutely that he has not. There is no question that a man can have a right of property in his productions so far as the law may choose to create one for him. But the first point at issue between many distinguished and powerful disputants is, whether he has a natural right.

Now, for me the matter is simplified by my believing that men, if they go down into their own minds and deal quite freely with their own consciousness, will find that they have not any natural rights at all. And as it so often happens with a difficult matter of dispute, so it happens here; the difficulty, the embarrassment, the need for drawing subtle distinctions and for devising subtle means of escape from them, when the right of property is under discussion, arises from one's having first built up the idea of natural right as a wall to run one's head against. An author has no natural right to a property in his production. But then neither has he a natural right to anything whatever which he may produce or acquire.

What is true is, that a man has a strong instinct making him seek to possess what he has produced or acquired, to have it at his own disposal; that he finds pleasure in so having it, and finds profit. The instinct is natural and salutary, although it may be over-stimulated and indulged to excess. One of the first objects of men, in combining themselves in society, has been to afford to the individual, in his pursuit of this instinct, the sanction and assistance of the laws, so far as may be consistent with the general advantage of the community.

The author, like other people, seeks the pleasure and the profit of having at his own disposal what he produces. Literary production, wherever it is sound, is its own exceeding great reward. But that does not destroy or diminish the author's desire and claim to be allowed to have at his disposal, like other people, that which he produces, and to be free to turn it to account. It happens that the thing which he produces is a thing hard for him to keep at his own disposal, easy for other people to appropriate. But then, on the other hand, he is an interesting producer, giving often a great deal of pleasure by what he produces, and not provoking Nemesis by any huge and immoderate profits on his production, even when it is suffered to be at his own disposal.

So society has taken the author under its protection, and has sanctioned, to a certain extent, his property in his work, and enabled him to have it at his own disposal. In England our laws give him the property in his work for forty-two years, or for his own life and seven years afterwards, whichever period is longest. In France, the law gives him the property in his work for his own life, and his widow's life, and for twenty years afterwards if he leave children; for ten years if he have other heirs. In Germany, the property in his work is for his life and thirty years afterwards. In Italy, for his life and forty years afterwards, with a further period during which a royalty has to be paid upon it to his heirs. In the United States, the author's property in his work is guaranteed for twenty-eight years from publication, with the right of renewal to himself, his wife, or his children, for fourteen years more. And this, though the author's production is a thing confessedly difficult to protect, and easy to appropriate. But it is possible to protect it; and so the author is suffered to enjoy the property in his production, to have it at his own disposal.

But is the author's production really property, ask some people; has he any natural right to it? Mr. Farrer, like so many other people, seems to be haunted by a metaphysical conception of *property in itself*,—a conception distinguishing between certain things, as belonging to the class of that which is property in itself, and certain other things, as belonging to the class of that which is not property in itself. Mr. Farrer's *dog*, his *place in the sun* at

Abinger, are of the class of property in itself; his *book*, if he produces one, is of the class of that which is not property in itself. Sir Louis Mallet is in the same order of ideas, when he insists that 'property arises from limitation of supply.' Property according to its essential nature, Sir Louis Mallet means, property in itself.

Let us beware of this metaphysical phantom of property in itself, which, like other metaphysical phantoms, is hollow and leads us to delusion. Property is the creation of law. It is effect given, by society and its laws, to that natural instinct in man which makes him seek to enjoy ownership in what he produces, acquires, or has. The effect is given because the instinct is natural, and because society, which makes the laws, is itself composed of men who feel the instinct. The instinct is natural, and in general society will comply with it. But there are certain cases in which society will not comply with it, or will comply with it in a very limited degree only. And what has determined society, in these cases, to refuse or greatly limit its compliance with the instinct of ownership, is the difficulty of giving effect to it, the disadvantage of trying to give effect to it in spite of such difficulty.

There is no property, people often say, in ideas uttered in conversation, in spoken words; and it is inferred that there ought to be no property in ideas and words when they are embodied in a book. But why is there no property in ideas uttered in conversation, and in spoken words, while there is property in ideas and words when they come in a book? A brilliant talker may very well have the instinct of ownership in his good sayings, and all the more if he must and can only talk them and not write them. He might be glad of power to prevent the appropriation of them by other people, to fix the conditions on which alone the appropriation should be allowed, and to derive profit from allowing it. Society, again, may well feel sympathy with his instinct of ownership, feel a disposition to assist and favour a production which gives it so much pleasure. But we are met by the *difficulty*, the insuperable difficulty, of giving effect to the producer's instinct of ownership in this case, of securing to him the disposal of his spoken ideas and words. Accordingly, effect is not given to it, and in such spoken ideas and words there is no property.

In other cases there is a partial and limited property given, and from the same reason,—from the difficulty of giving complete ownership. Game is an instance in point. A man breeds pheasants, rears them and feeds them, and he has a natural instinct to keep them in his entire possession, and at his own disposal. But the law will allow but a partial satisfaction to this instinct of his, and the moment his pheasants leave his land they may be taken by the person to whose ground they go. Of his chickens, meanwhile, a man retains ownership, even though they may pass over to his neighbour's field. Yet very likely he has bought the eggs of the pheasants and of the chickens alike, reared them both, fed them both, and feels the instinct and desire to claim them both alike as his property. But the law gives effect to this desire fully as regards the chickens, only partially as regards the pheasants. Why? Because of the far greater difficulty of giving full effect to it as regards the pheasants, and of the disadvantage which may arise from persisting in giving effect to it in spite of the difficulty. The law denies to a man the complete ownership of his pheasants, because they are difficult to keep at his own disposal, easy for other people to appropriate. And other people are more prone to appropriate them than the chickens, and more inclined to dispute his ownership of them, because of this very difficulty in maintaining it and facility in violating it. Even the partial ownership of his pheasants which the law does allow to a man, it has to fortify by special measures for its support; by making trespass in pursuit of game a different and more serious offence than common trespass. To gratify his instinct of ownership fully, to let a man have his pheasants at his entire disposal, the law would have to take more stringent and exceptional measures in his favour than it takes now ; and this every one feels to be out of the question. The law will certainly not do more for him than it does now; the only question is, whether it ought to do so much. To give even as much ownership in game as a man enjoys now, special measures in his favour are required, because his ownership meets with such great natural difficulties. So great are these difficulties, that the special measures to counteract them are far less likely to be reinforced than to be withdrawn.

And now to apply this to the question of copyright. The instinct of an author to desire ownership in his production, and advantage from that ownership, is natural. The author is an interesting person, and society may, and probably will, be even more ready, rather than less ready, to aid in giving effect to the instinct in his case than in the case of others, if it can be done without grave inconvenience. But there is difficulty in securing his ownership. The author's production is a production difficult to keep at his own disposal, easy for others to appropriate. His claim to some benefit of ownership, however, is generally admitted, and he has ownership given to him for a limited term of years. He finds a publisher, and in concert with him he exercises his owner-

s

ship; and the result in England of this concert between author and publisher is, that English books are exceedingly dear. A strong desire for cheaper books begins to be felt. Here is the real importance of Sir Louis Mallet's contention and of Mr. Farrer's. 'To Englishmen,' says Sir Louis Mallet, ' easy access to the contemporary literature of their own language is only possible on the condition of exile; England is the only country in which English books are scarce or dear.' 'Nothing can be more intolerable,' says Mr. Farrer, 'than a system of copyright-law under which the inhabitants of the mother-country, in which the books are produced, are the only persons in the world who are prevented from obtaining cheap editions of them.' An impatience, to which Mr. Farrer and Sir Louis Mallet here give utterance, an impatience at the dearness of English books, a desire to have them cheaper, has therefore to be added to the original difficulty of securing the author's ownership in a kind of production which is by nature hard to keep at his disposal, easy for others to appropriate. An increased difficulty of securing his ownership is the result.

The ingenious reasoning of many advocates of the rights of authors, and even the line taken by Mr. Froude in that instructive and interesting article on Copyright which he published in the *Edinburgh Review*, fail, it seems to me, to touch the point where the strength of their adversaries' case lies. Like their adversaries, they lodge themselves, stark and stiff, in the idea of 'property in itself.' Only, for them, an author's work is 'property in itself' just as much as his horse or his field; while, for their adversaries, his horse or his field is 'property in itself,' but his work is not. Let us grant that the adversaries are wrong, and that an author's work is 'property in itself' (whatever that may mean), just as much as his horse or his field. He has at any rate, we will suppose, the same instinct making him seek to have the ownership and profit of his work, as to have the ownership and profit of his horse or field. But what makes the law give him such full ownership as it does of his horse or field, is not, that the horse or field is 'property in itself;' it is, that to comply with his natural desire, and to secure him in his ownership, is in the case of the horse or field comparatively easy. And what makes the law give him a more limited ownership of his literary work, is not, that this work fails to prove its claim to be considered 'property in itself;' it is, that, in the case of his literary work, to secure him in his ownership is much more difficult. And suppose we add sufficiently to the difficulty, by the rise of a general impatience at the dearness of new books in England; of general irritation, at seeing that a work like Lord Macaulay's Life comes out at thirty-six shillings in England, while in France it would come out at eighteen francs, that a new novel by George Eliot costs a guinea and a half, while a new novel by George Sand costs three shillings; of general complaints that 'the inhabitants of the mother-country, in which the books are produced, are the only persons in the world who are prevented from obtaining cheap editions of them,'—suppose we add, I say, to the difficulty by all this, and you endanger the retention of even the right of ownership which the law secures to the author now. The advantage of complying with the author's instinct of ownership might be outweighed by the disadvantage of complying with it under such accumulated and immense difficulty.

But yet to secure, so far as without intolerable inconvenience it can be done, the benefits of ownership in his production to the author, every one, or almost every one, professes to desire. And in general, those who profess to desire this do really mean, I think, what they say; and there is no disposition in their minds to put the author off with benefits which are illusory. But Mr. Farrer and others propose,—no doubt without intending the poor author any harm,—a mode of benefit to him from his productions which does seem quite illusory. The proposal is to set all the world free to print and sell his work as soon as it appears, on condition of paying him a royalty of ten per cent. But both authors and publishers, and all who have the most experience in the matter, and the nearest interest, unite in saying that the author's benefit under this plan would be precarious and illusory. The poor man pursuing his ten per cent. over Great Britain and Ireland would be pitiable enough. But what shall we say of him pursuing his ten per cent. over all the British Dominions; what shall we say of him pursuing it, under an international copyright on this plan between all English-speaking people, over the United States of America? There are many objections to this plan of a royalty; but the decisive objection is, that whereas every one professes the wish not to take away from the author all substantial benefit from the sale of his work, this plan, in the opinion of those best able to judge, would take it away entirely.

The Royal Commission reported against this plan of a royalty, and in favour of continuing the present plan of securing by law to the author an ownership in his work for a limited term of years. The Commissioners have proposed what would, in my opinion, be a very great improvement upon the present arrangement. Instead of a copyright for forty-two years, or for life and seven years after, whichever period is longest, they propose to give, as in Germany, a copyright for the author's life and for thirty years after. But the principle is the same as in the arrangement of 1842, and there is no danger at present, in spite of Mr. Farrer's efforts, of the principle being departed from. Mr. Froude says truly that the course recommended by Mr. Farrer,—the withdrawal from the author, in effect, of the benefits of ownership in his work,—is a course which every single person practically connected with literature consents in condemning. He says truly that there is no agitation for it. He says truly that the press is silent about it, and that no complaints are heard from the public.

And yet the natural facts, in England as in France, are as Michel Lévy states them in his conversation with Madame Sand : there is a need for cheaper books the need will have to be satisfied, and it may be satisfied without loss to either author or publisher. What gives gravity to the dissatisfaction of Sir Louis Mallet and of Mr. Farrer with the actual course of the book-trade in England is, that the course of our book-trade goes counter to those natural facts. Sooner or later it will have to adjust itself to them, or there will be an explosion of discontent likely enough to sweep away copyright, and to destroy the author's benefit from his work by reducing it to some such illusory benefit as that offered by the royalty plan of Mr. Farrer. As our nation grows more civilised, as a real love of reading comes to prevail more widely, the system which keeps up the present exorbitant price of new books in England, the system of lending-libraries from which books are hired, will be seen to be, as it is, eccentric, artificial, and unsatisfactory in the highest degree. It is a machinery for the multiplication and protection of bad literature, and for keeping good books dear. In general, a book which is worth a man's reading is worth his possessing. The plan of having one's books from a lending-library leads to reading imperfectly and without discrimination, to glancing at books and not going through them, or rather to going through, for the most part, a quantity of the least profitable sort of books only,—novels,—and of but glancing at whatever is more serious. Every genuine reader will feel that the book he cares to read he cares to possess, and the number of genuine readers amongst us, in spite of all our shortcomings, is on the increase.

Mr. Froude, indeed, says, having the experience of an editor's shelves before his eyes, that instead of desiring the possession of more books than one has, one might rather desire not to possess half of those which one has now. But the books he means are just those which a genuine reader would never think of buying, and which yet are shot upon us now in profusion by the lending-libraries. Mr. Froude says, again, that new books are not the best books, and that old books, which are best, are to be bought cheap. True, old books of surpassing value are to be bought cheap; but there are good new books, too, and good new books have a stimulus and an interest peculiar to themselves, and the reader will not be content to forego them. Mr. Herbert Spencer may tell him, that to desire the possession of good new books, when he is not rich, is merely the common case of the poor desiring to possess what is accessible to the rich only; that it is as if he wanted fine horses, and the best champagne, and hothouse flowers, and strawberries at Christmas. But the answer is that the good new books, unlike the horses and champagne, may be brought within his reach without loss to the vendor, and that it is only the eccentric, artificial, and highly unsatisfactory system of our book-trade which prevents it.

The three-shilling book is our great want,—the book at three shillings or half-a-crown, like the books of the *format Lévy*, shapely and seemly, and as acceptable to the eye as the far dearer books which we have now. The price proposed will perfectly allow of this. The French books of the *format Lévy*, and the French books in octavo, are as shapely and seemly, as acceptable to the eye, as the corresponding English books at double and treble their price. The two octavo volumes of Madame de Rémusat's Memoirs, in French, cost but twelve shillings, yet they make a handsomer book than the two octavo volumes of the same work in English, which cost thirty-two. A cheap literature hideous and ignoble of aspect, like the tawdry novels which flare in the book-shelves of our railway-stations, and which seem designed, as so much else that is produced for the use of our middle-class seems designed, for people with a low standard of life, is not what is wanted. A sense of beauty and fitness ought to be satisfied in the form and aspect of the books we read, as well as by their contents. To have the contents offered one for next to nothing, but in hideous and ignoble form and aspect, is not what one desires. A man would willingly pay higher, but in the measure of his means, for what he values, in order to have it in worthy form. But our present prices are prohibitive. The taste for beautiful books is a charming and humane taste for a rich man, though really, as has been already said, our ordinary dear books gratify this taste not a bit better than the French cheaper ones. However, the taste for beautiful books requires expense, no doubt, to be fully gratified; and in large paper copies and exquisite bindings the rich man may gratify it still, as he still gratifies it in France, even when we have reformed our book-trade as the French have reformed theirs. For reforming ours, the signal innovation necessary, as in France, is the three-shilling book; although, of course, the price of our new works in octavo at sixteen or eighteen shillings a volume would also have to be reduced in proportion. If nothing of this kind is done, if the system of our book-trade remains as it is, dissatisfaction, not loud and active at present,—I grant that to Mr. Froude,—will grow and stir more and more, and will certainly end by menacing, in spite of whatever conclusion the Royal Commission may now adopt and proclaim, the proprietary right of the author.

The doctrine of M. Michel Lévy respecting the book-trade, and what I have been now saying about our book-trade at home, have their application in America also, and I must end with a few words concerning the book-trade of the United States. Indeed, one is invited by the Americans themselves to do so, for the famous publishers in New York, the Messrs. Harper, have addressed to the authors and publishers of this country a proposal for an International Conference on Copyright. Mr. Conant, who is understood to be connected with the publishing house of the Messrs. Harper, has given in an English magazine an exposition of American opinion on the matter; and an Englishman of legal training and great acuteness, who signs himself 'C.,' but whom we may, I believe, without indiscretion, name as Mr. Leonard Courtney, has commented on Mr. Conant's exposition.

The Americans, as is well known, have at present (to quote the words of an American, Mr. George Putnam, who has published on this question of copyright a pamphlet very temperate and, in general, very judicious) 'no regulation to prevent the use, without remuneration, of the literary property of foreign authors.' Mr. Putnam adds: 'The United States is, therefore, at present the only country, itself possessing a literature of importance, and making a large use of the literature of the world, which has done nothing to recognise and protect by law the rights of foreign authors of whose property it is enjoying the benefit, or to obtain a similar recognition and protection for its own authors abroad.'

The Americans, some of them, as is also well known, defend this state of things by adopting the cry of 'free books for free men.' A Conference held at Philadelphia, in 1872, passed resolutions declaring that, 'thought, when given to the world, is, as light, free to all;' and, moreover, that 'the good of our whole people, and the safety of our republican institutions, demand that books shall not be made too costly for the multitude by giving the power to foreign authors to fix their price here as well as abroad.'

Mr. Conant, in his representation to the English public of the case of the American public, adopts these Philadelphian ideas in principle. But he maintains that in practice the American publishers have generously waived their right to act on them, and he carries the war into the enemy's country. He says for himself and his countrymen : 'We are keenly alive to the necessity of the general diffusion of intelligence. Upon it depends the perpetuity of our republican form of government. Europe is constantly pouring upon our shores a mighty deluge of ignorance and superstition. We welcome here the poor, the outcasts of every land. There is a wide-spread feeling that the Old World, which contributes this mass of ignorance and superstition to our population, should also contribute to the alleviation of the resulting ills.' Mr. Conant alleges that the concession in past times of a copyright to English authors 'would have retarded the progress of American culture at least half a century, and delayed that wide-spread intellectual development from which English authors reap so large a benefit.'

And yet nevertheless, says this good Mr. Conant, 'the course of American publishers, pursued for many years, towards foreign men of letters, shows that they have no disposition to take advantage of the absence of international copyright.' He declares: 'As for English authors, they have already learned that their interests are quite safe in the hands of "Yankee pirates," as some of your writers still persist in calling the men who for years have conducted the publishing business of this country with the most scrupulous regard for the rights of foreign authors. Few English people, I think, have any notion of the amount of money paid to British authors by American publishers. Those authors whose books have been reprinted here without compensation to the author, may rest assured that this was owing to the fact that the sale was not remunerative here, and that international copyright will not make it larger.' On the other hand: 'While for twenty-five years past British authors have enjoyed all the material advantages of copyright in this country, American books have been reprinted in England by the thousand, without compensation to the authors.' And therefore, adds Mr. Conant, 'in view of these facts, an American may be pardoned for indulging in a quiet laugh at the lofty tone which the Royal Commissioners on Copyright assume in their solemn arraignment of the United States for refusing to grant protection to English authors.'

And so the tables are fairly turned upon us. Not only

have English authors no reason to complain of America, but American authors have great reason to complain of England.

An English author, as he reads Mr. Conant, will by turns be inclined to laugh and to be indignant. Mr. Leonard Courtney handles Mr. Conant's statement very scornfully and severely. For myself, I am of a gentle disposition, and I am disposed, in reading Mr. Conant in *Macmillan's Magazine,* to ask him before all things Figaro's question : *Qui est-ce qu'on trompe ici* ?—Who is it that is being taken in here ? At the Philadelphia Conference, Mr. Conant's statement would have been quite in place ; but why he should address it to the British public passes my comprehension. Our British middle class, no doubt, like the great middle-class public of the United States, likes to have its defective practice covered by an exhibition of fine sentiments. But it is our own defective practice that we seek to cover by the exhibition of fine sentiments ;—as, for instance, when we left Denmark in the lurch after all our admonitions and threatenings to Germany, we assured one another that the whole world admired our moral attitude. But it gives us no pleasure or comfort to see other people's defective practice, by which we are smarting, covered with an exhibition of fine sentiments. And so, as I peruse Mr.

Conant, with Figaro I inquire in bewilderment: 'Who is it that is being taken in here?' We know perfectly well the real facts of the case, and that they are not as Mr. Conant puts them; and we have no interest in getting them dressed up to look otherwise than as they are. Our interest is to see them as they really are; for as they really are, they are in our favour.

If American authors have not copyright here in England, whose fault is that? It is the fault of America herself, who again and again has refused to entertain the question of international copyright. Again and again, in Mr. Conant's own statement of facts, appears the proposal, on the part of England, of an international copyright; and again and again the end of it is, 'the report was adverse,' 'no action was taken,' 'shelved,' ' more pressing matters crowded it out of sight.' If Englishmen suffer by having no copyright in America, they have the American government and people to thank for it. If Americans suffer by having no copyright in England, they have only to thank themselves.

But is it true that American authors have no copyright in England? It is so far from being true, that an American has only to visit England when he publishes his book here,—or even, I believe, has only to cross the border into Canada,—in order to have copyright in his work in

England. Mr. Motley told me himself that in this way he had acquired copyright in England for his valuable histories. Mr. Henry James gets it in the same way at this moment for those charming novels of his which we are all reading. But no English author can acquire copyright in the United States.

As to the liberal payment given at present, without copyright, by American publishers to English authors, it is more difficult to speak securely. Certainly it is far too much to say of British authors in general, that they 'for at least twenty-five years past have enjoyed all the material advantages of copyright in America;' or that they 'have learned that their interests are quite safe in the hands of American publishers.' Considerable sums have, no doubt, been paid. Men of science, such as Professor Huxley and Professor Tyndall, are especially mentioned as satisfied with the remuneration voluntarily accorded to them by the American publishers; and indeed, to judge by the success of their American dealings, it seems that these inheritors of the future, the men of science, besides having their hold upon the world which is to come, have their hold likewise, lucky fellows, upon the world which now is! Men of letters have not been so fortunate; and the list, given by Mr. Conant, of those to whom a surprising amount of money is paid from America, is to be received with caution. Mr. Tennyson is mentioned; but I hear from the best authority that in truth Mr. Tennyson has received little or nothing from the sale of his works in America. One can at least speak for oneself; and certainly I have never received, from first to last, a hundred pounds from America, though my books have been, I believe, much reprinted there. Mr. Conant will probably say that I am one of those authors 'whose sale is not remunerative,' and does not come to much either there or here. And perhaps according to the grand scale by which he weighs things, this may very well be true. Only, if I had not received more than a hundred pounds here or in America either, during the quarter of a century that I have gone up and down, as the mockers say, preaching sweetness and light, one could never have managed to drag on, even in Grub Street, for all these years.

The truth is, the interests of British authors in general cannot well be safe in America, so long as the publishers there are free to reprint whom they please, and to pay, of the authors they reprint, whom they please, and at what rate they please. The interests of English authors will never be safe in America until the community, as a community, gets the sense, in a higher degree than it has it now, for acting with delicacy. It is the sense of

T

delicacy which has to be appealed to, not the sense of honesty. Englishmen are fond of making the American appropriation of their books a question of honesty. They call the appropriation stealing. If an English author drops his handkerchief in Massachusetts, they say, the natives may not go off with it ; but if he drops his poem, they may. This style of talking is exaggerated and false. There is a breach of delicacy in reprinting the foreigner's poem without his consent, there is no breach of honesty. But a finely touched nature, in men or nations, will respect in itself the sense of delicacy not less than the sense of honesty. The Latin nations, the French and Italians, have that instinctive recognition of the charm of art and letters, which disposes them, as a community, to care for the interests of artists and authors, and to treat them with delicacy. In Germany learning is very highly esteemed, and both the government and the community are inclined to treat the interests of authors considerately and delicately. Aristocracies, again, are brought up in elegance and refinement, and are taught to believe that art and letters go for much in making the beauty and grace of human life, and perhaps they do believe it. At any rate, they feel bound to show the disposition to treat the interests of artists and authors with delicacy ; and shown it the aristocratic government and parliament of England have. We must not indeed expect them to take the trouble for art and letters which the government of France will take. We must not expect of them the zeal that procured for French authors the Belgian Copyright Treaty of 1854, and stopped those Brussels reprints which drove poor Balzac to despair. Neither in India, nor in Canada, nor yet in the United States, has our aristocratic government interposed on behalf of the author with this energy. They do not think him and his concerns of importance enough to deserve it. Still, they feel a disposition to treat his interests with consideration and with delicacy; and, so far as the thing depends on themselves, they show them.

The United States are a great middle-class community of our own race,—free from many obstructions which cramp the middle class in our own country, and with a supply of humane individuals sown over the land, who keep increasing their numbers and gaining in courage and in strength, and more and more make themselves felt in the press and periodical literature of America. Still, on the whole, the spirit of the American community and government is the spirit, I suppose, of a middle-class society of our race; and this is not a spirit of delicacy. One could not say that in their public acts the United

States showed, in general, a spirit of delicacy. Certainly they have not shown that spirit in dealing with authors,— even with their own. They deal with authors, domestic and foreign, much as Manchester, perhaps, might be disposed, if left to itself, to deal with them; as if, provided a sharp bargain was made, and *a good thing*, as the phrase is, was got out of it, that was all which could be desired, and the community might exult. The worship of sharp bargains is fatal to delicacy. Nor is the missing grace restored by accompanying the sharp bargain with an exhibition of fine sentiments.

As the great American community becomes more truly and thoroughly civilised, it will certainly learn to add to its many and great virtues the spirit of delicacy. And English authors will be gainers by it. At present they are gainers from another cause. It appears that till lately there was an understanding amongst American publishers, that, when one publisher had made terms with an English author for the republication of his work in America, the rest should respect the agreement, and should leave their colleague in possession of the work. But about two years and a half ago, says Mr. Conant, certain parties began to set at naught this law of trade-courtesy. Certain firms 'began to republish the works of foreign authors, paying nothing for the privilege, and bringing out absurdly cheap editions right on the heels of the authorised reprint, which had cost a large outlay for priority and expense of publication.' The ruinous competition thus produced has had the effect, Mr. Putnam tells us in his pamphlet, of 'pointing out the absurdity of the present condition of literary property, and emphasising the need of an international copyright.' It has had the effect, he says, of 'influencing a material modification of opinion on the part of publishers who have in years past opposed an international copyright as either inexpedient or unnecessary, but who are now quoted as ready to give their support to any practicable and equitable measure that may be proposed.' Nothing could be more satisfactory.

Accordingly, it is now suggested from America that an international copyright treaty should be proposed by the United States to Great Britain, and, as a first step, that 'a Commission or Conference of American citizens and British subjects, in which the United States and Great Britain shall be equally represented, be appointed respectively by the American Secretary of State and by the British Secretary of State for Foreign Affairs, who shall be invited jointly to consider and present the details of a treaty.'

The details are reserved for the Conference; but it is

no secret what the main lines of such a treaty, if it is to be accepted in America, must be. The American author will be allowed, on registering his work, to have copyright in England, and the English author to have copyright in the United States. But the foreigner's work must be manufactured and published in the country, and by a subject or citizen of the country, in which it is registered. The English author's book, therefore, to be protected in America, must be manufactured and published in America as well as in England. He will not be allowed to print and publish his book in England only, and to send his copies over to the United States for sale. The main object, I think, of Mr. Conant's exposition, is to make it clear to us on the English side of the water that from this condition the Americans will not suffer themselves to be moved.

English publishers and authors seem inclined to cry out that such a condition is an interference with the author's 'freedom of contract.' But then they take their stand on the ground that an author's production is 'property in itself,' and that one of the incidents of 'property in itself' is to confer on its possessor the right to 'freedom of contract' respecting it. I, however, who recognise natural difficulty as setting bounds to ownership, must ask whether, supposing the English author's need for copyright in America to be pressing, he can reasonably expect to be admitted to copyright there without this condition.

Mr. Froude and Mr. Leonard Courtney both of them seem to think that the question of international copyright is not at all pressing. They say that opinion in America is slowly ripening for some better and more favourable settlement of copyright than any settlement which America is now likely to accept; and that, meanwhile, English authors may be well enough content with their present receipts from American publishers, and had better let things stay as they are.

A few English authors may, perhaps, be content enough with their present receipts from America, but to suppose that English authors in general may well be so content, is, I think, a very hazardous supposition. That, however, is of little importance. The important question is, whether American opinion, if we give it time, is likely to cease insisting on the condition that English books, in order to acquire copyright in America, must be manufactured and published there; is likely to recognise the English author and publisher as Siamese twins, one of whom is not to be imported without importing the other. Is there any chance, in short, of the Americans, accustomed to cheap English books, submitting to that dearness of English books which is brought about in England by what, in spite of all my attachment to certain English publishers, I must call our highly eccentric, artificial, and unsatisfactory system of book-trade? I confess I see no chance of it whatever. There is a mountain of natural difficulty in the way, there is the irresistible opposition of things.

Here, then, where lies the real gist of his contention, I am after all at one with Mr. Conant. The Americans ought not to submit to our absurd system of dear books. I am sure they will not; and, as a lover of civilisation, I should be sorry, though I am an author, if they did. I hope the Americans will give us copyright. But I hope also, that they will stick to Michel Lévy's excellent doctrine: 'Cheap books are a necessity, and a necessity which need bring, moreover, no loss to either authors or publishers.'

PREFACE TO FIRST EDITION OF POEMS.
(1853.)

In two small volumes of Poems, published anonymously, one in 1849, the other in 1852, many of the poems which compose the present volume have already appeared. The rest are now published for the first time.

I have, in the present collection, omitted the poem from which the volume published in 1852 took its title. I have done so, not because the subject of it was a Sicilian Greek born between two and three thousand years ago, although many persons would think this a sufficient reason. Neither have I done so because I had, in my own opinion, failed in the delineation which I intended to effect. I intended to delineate the feelings of one of the last of the Greek religious philosophers, one of the family of Orpheus and Musæus, having survived his fellows, living on into a time when the habits of Greek thought and feeling had begun fast to change, character to dwindle, the influence of the Sophists to prevail. Into the feelings of a man so situated there entered much that we are accustomed to consider as exclusively modern; how much, the fragments of Empedocles himself which remain to us are sufficient at least to indicate. What those who are familiar only with the great monuments of early Greek genius suppose to be its exclusive characteristics, have disappeared; the calm, the cheerfulness, the disinterested objectivity have disappeared; the dialogue of the mind with itself has commenced; modern problems have presented themselves; we hear already the doubts, we witness the discouragement, of Hamlet and of Faust.

The representation of such a man's feelings must be interesting, if consistently drawn. We all naturally take pleasure, says Aristotle, in any imitation or representation whatever; this is the basis of our love of poetry; and we take pleasure in them, he adds, because all knowledge is naturally agreeable to us; not to the philosopher only, but to mankind at large. Every representation, therefore, which is consistently drawn may be supposed to be interesting, inasmuch as it gratifies this natural interest in knowledge of all kinds. What is *not* interesting, is that which does not add to our knowledge of any kind; that which is vaguely conceived and loosely drawn; a representation which is general, indeterminate, and faint, instead of being particular, precise, and firm.

Any accurate representation may therefore be expected to be interesting; but, if the representation be a poetical one, more than this is demanded. It is demanded, not only that it shall interest, but also that it shall inspirit and rejoice the reader; that it shall convey a charm, and infuse delight. For the Muses, as Hesiod says, were born that they might be 'a forgetfulness of evils, and a truce from cares:' and it is not enough that the poet should add to the knowledge of men, it is required of him also that he should add to their happiness. 'All art,' says Schiller, 'is dedicated to Joy, and there is no higher and no more serious problem, than how to make men happy. The right art is that alone, which creates the highest enjoyment.'

A poetical work, therefore, is not yet justified when it has been shown to be an accurate, and therefore interesting representation; it has to be shown also that it is a representation from which men can derive enjoyment. In presence of the most tragic circumstances, represented in a work of art, the feeling of enjoyment, as is well known, may still subsist; the representation of the most utter calamity, of the liveliest anguish, is not sufficient to destroy it; the more tragic the situation, the deeper becomes the enjoyment; and the situation is more tragic in proportion as it becomes more terrible.

What then are the situations, from the representation of which, though accurate, no poetical enjoyment can be derived? They are those in which the suffering finds no vent in action; in which a continuous state of mental distress is prolonged, unrelieved by incident, hope, or resistance; in which there is everything to be endured, nothing to be done. In such situations there is inevitably something morbid, in the description of them something monotonous. When they occur in actual life, they are painful, not tragic; the representation of them in poetry is painful also.

To this class of situations, poetically faulty as it appears to me, that of Empedocles, as I have endeavoured to represent him, belongs; and I have therefore excluded the poem from the present collection.

And why, it may be asked, have I entered into this explanation respecting a matter so unimportant as the admission or exclusion of the poem in question? I have done so, because I was anxious to avow that the sole reason for its exclusion was that which has been stated above; and that it has not been excluded in deference to the opinion which many critics of the present day appear to entertain against subjects chosen from distant times and countries : against the choice, in short, of any subjects but modern ones.

'The poet,' it is said,[1] and by an intelligent critic, 'the poet who would really fix the public attention must leave the exhausted past, and draw his subjects from matters of present import, and *therefore* both of interest and novelty.'

Now this view I believe to be completely false. It is worth examining, inasmuch as it is a fair sample of a class of critical dicta everywhere current at the present day, having a philosophical form and air, but no real basis in fact ; and which are calculated to vitiate the judgment of readers of poetry, while they exert, so far as they are adopted, a misleading influence on the practice of those who make it.

What are the eternal objects of poetry, among all nations, and at all times? They are actions ; human actions ; possessing an inherent interest in themselves, and which are to be communicated in an interesting manner by the art of the poet. Vainly will the latter imagine that he has everything in his own power ; that he can make an intrinsically inferior action equally delightful

---

[1] In the *Spectator* of April 2, 1853. The words quoted were not used with reference to poems of mine.

with a more excellent one by his treatment of it. He may indeed compel us to admire his skill, but his work will possess, within itself, an incurable defect.

The poet, then, has in the first place to select an excellent action; and what actions are the most excellent? Those, certainly, which most powerfully appeal to the great primary human affections: to those elementary feelings which subsist permanently in the race, and which are independent of time. These feelings are permanent and the same; that which interests them is permanent and the same also. The modernness or antiquity of an action, therefore, has nothing to do with its fitness for poetical representation; this depends upon its inherent qualities. To the elementary part of our nature, to our passions, that which is great and passionate is eternally interesting; and interesting solely in proportion to its greatness and to its passion. A great human action of a thousand years ago is more interesting to it than a smaller human action of to-day, even though upon the representation of this last the most consummate skill may have been expended, and though it has the advantage of appealing by its modern language, familiar manners, and contemporary allusions, to all our transient feelings and interests. These, however, have no right to demand of a poetical work that it shall satisfy them; their claims are to be directed elsewhere. Poetical works belong to the domain of our permanent passions; let them interest these, and the voice of all subordinate claims upon them is at once silenced.

Achilles, Prometheus, Clytemnestra, Dido,—what modern poem presents personages as interesting, even to us moderns, as these personages of an 'exhausted past?' We have the domestic epic dealing with the details of modern life which pass daily under our eyes; we have poems representing modern personages in contact with the problems of modern life, moral, intellectual, and social; these works have been produced by poets the most distinguished of their nation and time; yet I fearlessly assert that Hermann and Dorothea, Childe Harold, Jocelyn, the Excursion, leave the reader cold in comparison with the effect produced upon him by the latter books of the Iliad, by the Oresteia, or by the episode of Dido. And why is this? Simply because in the three last-named cases the action is greater, the personages nobler, the situations more intense: and this is the true basis of the interest in a poetical work, and this alone.

It may be urged, however, that past actions may be interesting in themselves, but that they are not to be adopted by the modern poet, because it is impossible for him to have them clearly present to his own mind, and he cannot therefore feel them deeply, nor represent them forcibly. But this is not necessarily the case. The externals of a past action, indeed, he cannot know with the precision of a contemporary; but his business is with its essentials. The outward man of Œdipus or of Macbeth, the houses in which they lived, the ceremonies of their courts, he cannot accurately figure to himself; but neither do they essentially concern him. His business is with their inward man; with their feelings and behaviour in certain tragic situations, which engage their passions as men; these have in them nothing local and casual; they are as accessible to the modern poet as to a contemporary.

The date of an action, then, signifies nothing; the action itself, its selection and construction, this is what is all-important. This the Greeks understood far more clearly than we do. The radical difference between their poetical theory and ours consists, as it appears to me, in this: that, with them, the poetical character of the action in itself, and the conduct of it, was the first consideration; with us, attention is fixed mainly on the value of the separate thoughts and images which occur in the treatment of an action. They regarded the whole; we regard the parts. With them, the action predominated over the expression of it; with us, the expression predominates over the action. Not that they failed in expression, or were inattentive to it; on the contrary, they are the highest models of expression, the unapproached masters of the *grand style*. But their expression is so excellent because it is so admirably kept in its right degree of prominence; because it is so simple and so well subordinated; because it draws its force directly from the pregnancy of the matter which it conveys. For what reason was the Greek tragic poet confined to so limited a range of subjects? Because there are so few actions which unite in themselves, in the highest degree, the conditions of excellence: and it was not thought that on any but an excellent subject could an excellent poem be constructed. A few actions, therefore, eminently adapted for tragedy, maintained almost exclusive possession of the Greek tragic stage. Their significance appeared inexhaustible; they were as permanent problems, perpetually offered to the genius of every fresh poet. This too is the reason of what appears to us moderns a certain baldness of expression in Greek tragedy; of the triviality with which we often reproach the remarks of the chorus, where it takes part in the dialogue: that the action itself, the situation of Orestes, or Merope, or Alcmæon, was to stand the central point of interest, unforgotten, absorbing, principal; that no accessories were for a moment to distract the spectator's attention from this; that the tone of the parts was to be perpetually kept down, in order not to impair the grandiose effect of the whole. The terrible old mythic story on which the drama was founded stood, before he entered the theatre, traced in its bare outlines upon the spectator's mind; it stood in his memory, as a group of statuary, faintly seen, at the end of a long and dark vista: then came the poet, embodying outlines, developing situations, not a word wasted, not a sentiment capriciously thrown in: stroke upon stroke, the drama proceeded: the light deepened upon the group; more and more it revealed itself to the riveted gaze of the spectator: until at last, when the final words were spoken, it stood before him in broad sunlight, a model of immortal beauty.

This was what a Greek critic demanded; this was what a Greek poet endeavoured to effect. It signified nothing to what time an action belonged. We do not find that the Persæ occupied a particularly high rank among the dramas of Æschylus, because it represented a matter of contemporary interest; this was not what a cultivated Athenian required. He required that the permanent elements of his nature should be moved; and dramas of which the action, though taken from a long-distant mythic time, yet was calculated to accomplish this in a higher degree than that of the Persæ, stood higher in his estimation accordingly. The Greeks felt, no doubt, with their exquisite sagacity of taste, that an action of present times was too near them, too much mixed up with what was accidental and passing, to form a sufficiently grand, detached, and self-subsistent object for a tragic poem. Such objects belonged to the domain of the comic poet, and of the lighter kinds of poetry. For the more serious kinds, for *pragmatic* poetry, to use an excellent expression of Polybius, they were more difficult and severe in the range of subjects which they permitted. Their theory and practice alike, the admirable treatise of Aristotle, and the unrivalled works of their poets, exclaim with a thousand tongues—'All depends upon the subject; choose a fitting action, penetrate yourself with the feeling of its situations; this done, everything else will follow.'

But for all kinds of poetry alike there was one point on which they were rigidly exacting; the adaptability of the subject to the kind of poetry selected, and the careful construction of the poem.

How different a way of thinking from this is ours! We can hardly at the present day understand what Menander meant, when he told a man who enquired as to the progress of his comedy that he had finished it, not having yet written a single line, because he had constructed the action of it in his mind. A modern critic would have assured him that the merit of his piece depended on the brilliant things which arose under his pen as he went along. We have poems which seem to exist merely for the sake of single lines and passages; not for the sake of producing any total impression. We have critics who seem to direct their attention merely to detached expressions, to the language about the action, not to the action itself. I verily think that the majority of them do not in their hearts believe that there is such a thing as a total impression to be derived from a poem at all, or to be demanded from a poet; they think the term a commonplace of metaphysical criticism. They will permit the poet to select any action he pleases, and to suffer that action to go as it will, provided he gratifies them with occasional bursts of fine writing, and with a shower of isolated thoughts and images. That is, they permit him to leave their poetical sense ungratified, provided that he gratifies their rhetorical sense and their curiosity. Of his neglecting to gratify these, there is little danger. He needs rather to be warned against the danger of attempting to gratify these alone; he needs rather to be perpetually reminded to prefer his action to everything else; so to treat this, as to permit its inherent excellences to develope themselves, without interruption from the intrusion of his personal peculiarities; most fortunate, when he most entirely succeeds in effacing himself, and in enabling a noble action to subsist as it did in nature.

But the modern critic not only permits a false practice; he absolutely prescribes false aims.—'A true allegory of the state of one's own mind in a representative history,' the poet is told, 'is perhaps the highest thing that one can attempt in the way of poetry.' And accordingly he attempts it. An allegory of the state of one's own mind, the highest problem of an art which imitates actions! No assuredly, it is not, it never can be so: no great poetical work has ever been produced with such an aim. Faust itself, in which something of the kind is attempted, wonderful passages as it contains, and in spite of the unsurpassed beauty of the scenes which relate to Margaret, Faust itself, judged as a whole, and judged strictly as a poetical work, is defective: its illustrious author, the greatest poet of modern times, the greatest critic of all times, would have been the first to acknowledge it; he only defended his work, indeed, by asserting it to be 'something incommensurable.'

The confusion of the present times is great, the multitude of voices counselling different things bewildering, the number of existing works capable of attracting a young writer's attention and of becoming his models, immense. What he wants is a hand to guide him through the confusion, a voice to prescribe to him the aim which he should keep in view, and to explain to him that the value of the literary works which offer themselves to his attention is relative to their power of helping him forward on his road towards this aim. Such a guide the English writer at the present day will nowhere find. Failing this, all that can be looked for, all indeed that can be desired, is, that his attention should be fixed on excellent models; that he may reproduce, at any rate, something of their excellence, by penetrating himself with their works and by catching their spirit, if he cannot be taught to produce what is excellent independently.

Foremost among these models for the English writer stands Shakespeare : a name the greatest perhaps of all poetical names ; a name never to be mentioned without reverence. I will venture, however, to express a doubt, whether the influence of his works, excellent and fruitful for the readers of poetry, for the great majority, has been of unmixed advantage to the writers of it. Shakespeare indeed chose excellent subjects ; the world could afford no better than Macbeth, or Romeo and Juliet, or Othello ; he had no theory respecting the necessity of choosing subjects of present import, or the paramount interest attaching to allegories of the state of one's own mind; like all great poets, he knew well what constituted a poetical action; like them, wherever he found such an action, he took it; like them, too, he found his best in past times. But to these general characteristics of all great poets he added a special one of his own; a gift, namely, of happy, abundant, and ingenious expression, eminent and unrivalled: so eminent as irresistibly to strike the attention first in him, and even to throw into comparative shade his other excellences as a poet. Here has been the mischief. These other excellences were his fundamental excellences *as a poet*; what distinguishes the artist from the mere amateur, says Goethe, is *Architonicè* in the highest sense; that power of execution, which creates, forms, and constitutes: not the profoundness of single thoughts, not the richness of imagery, not the abundance of illustration. But these attractive accessories of a poetical work being more easily seized than the spirit of the whole, and these accessories being possessed by Shakespeare in an unequalled degree, a young writer having recourse to Shakespeare as his model runs great risk of being vanquished and absorbed by them, and, in consequence, of reproducing, according to the measure of his power, these, and these alone. Of this preponderating quality of Shakespeare's genius, accordingly, almost the whole of modern English poetry has, it appears to me, felt the influence. To the exclusive attention on the part of his imitators to this it is in a great degree owing, that of the majority of modern poetical works the details alone are valuable, the composition worthless. In reading them one is perpetually reminded of that terrible sentence on a modern French poet :—*Il dit tout ce qu'il veut, mais malheureusement il n'a rien à dire.*

Let me give an instance of what I mean. I will take it from the works of the very chief among those who seem to have been formed in the school of Shakespeare : of one whose exquisite genius and pathetic death render him for ever interesting. I will take the poem of Isabella, or the Pot of Basil, by Keats. I choose this rather than the Endymion, because the latter work, (which a modern critic has classed with the Fairy Queen !) although undoubtedly there blows through it the breath of genius, is yet as a whole so utterly incoherent, as not strictly to merit the name of a poem at all. The poem of Isabella, then, is a perfect treasure-house of graceful and felicitous words and images : almost in every stanza there occurs one of those vivid and picturesque turns of expression, by which the object is made to flash upon the eye of the mind, and which thrill the reader with a sudden delight. This one short poem contains, perhaps, a greater number of happy single expressions which one could quote than all the extant tragedies of Sophocles. But the action, the story? The action in itself is an excellent one; but so feebly is it conceived by the poet, so loosely constructed, that the effect produced by it, in and for itself, is absolutely null. Let the reader, after he has finished the poem of Keats, turn to the same story in the Decameron: he will then feel how pregnant and interesting the same action has become in the hands of a great artist, who above all things delineates his object; who subordinates expression to that which it is designed to express.

I have said that the imitators of Shakespeare, fixing their attention on his wonderful gift of expression, have directed their imitation to this, neglecting his other excellences. These excellences, the fundamental excellences of poetical art, Shakespeare no doubt possessed them,—possessed many of them in a splendid degree; but it may perhaps be doubted whether even he himself did not sometimes give scope to his faculty of expression to the prejudice of a higher poetical duty. For we must never forget that Shakespeare is the great poet he is from his skill in discerning and firmly conceiving an excellent action, from his power of intensely feeling a situation, of intimately associating himself with a character; not from his gift of expression, which rather even leads him astray, degenerating sometimes into a fondness for curiosity of expression, into an irritability of fancy, which seems to make it impossible for him to say a thing plainly, even when the press of the action demands the very directest language, or its level character the very simplest. Mr. Hallam, than whom it is impossible to find a saner and more judicious critic, has had the courage (for at the present day it needs courage) to remark, how extremely and faultily difficult Shakespeare's language often is. It is so: you may find main scenes in some of his greatest tragedies, King Lear for instance, where the language is so artificial, so curiously tortured, and so difficult, that every speech has to be read two or three times before its meaning can be comprehended. This over-curiousness of expression is indeed but the excessive employment of a wonderful gift,—of the power of saying a thing in a happier way than any other man; nevertheless, it is carried so far that one understands what M. Guizot meant, when he said that Shakespeare appears in his language to have tried all styles except that of simplicity. He has not the severe and scrupulous self-restraint of the ancients, partly no doubt, because he had a far less cultivated and exacting audience. He has indeed a far wider range than they had, a far richer fertility of thought; in this respect he rises above them. In his strong conception of his subject, in the genuine way in which he is penetrated with it, he resembles them, and is unlike the moderns. But in the accurate limitation of it, the conscientious rejection of superfluities, the simple and rigorous development of it from the first line of his work to the last, he falls below them, and comes nearer to the moderns. In his chief works, besides what he has of his own, he has the elementary soundness of the ancients; he has their important action and their large and broad manner; but he has not their purity of method. He is therefore a less safe model; for what he has of his own is personal, and inseparable from his own rich nature; it may be imitated and exaggerated, it cannot be learned or applied as an art. He is above all suggestive; more valuable, therefore, to young writers as men than as artists. But clearness of arrangement, rigour of development, simplicity of style,—these may to a certain extent be learned; and these may, I am convinced, be learned best from the ancients, who, although infinitely less suggestive than Shakespeare, are thus, to the artist, more instructive.

What then, it will be asked, are the ancients to be

our sole models? the ancients with their comparatively narrow range of experience, and their widely different circumstances? Not, certainly, that which is narrow in the ancients, nor that in which we can no longer sympathise. An action like the action of the Antigone of Sophocles, which turns upon the conflict between the heroine's duty to her brother's corpse and that to the laws of her country, is no longer one in which it is possible that we should feel a deep interest. I am speaking too, it will be remembered, not of the best sources of intellectual stimulus for the general reader, but of the best models of instruction for the individual writer. This last may certainly learn of the ancients, better than anywhere else, three things which it is vitally important for him to know :—the all-importance of the choice of a subject; the necessity of accurate construction; and the subordinate character of expression. He will learn from them how unspeakably superior is the effect of the one moral impression left by a great action treated as a whole, to the effect produced by the most striking single thought or by the happiest image. As he penetrates into the spirit of the great classical works, as he becomes gradually aware of their intense significance, their noble simplicity, and their calm pathos, he will be convinced that it is this effect, unity and profoundness of moral impression, at which the ancient poets aimed; that it is this which constitutes the grandeur of their works, and which makes them immortal. He will desire to direct his own efforts towards producing the same effect. Above all, he will deliver himself from the jargon of modern criticism, and escape the danger of producing poetical works conceived in the spirit of the passing time, and which partake of its transitoriness.

The present age makes great claims upon us; we owe it service, it will not be satisfied without our admiration. I know not how it is, but their commerce with the ancients appears to me to produce, in those who constantly practise it, a steadying and composing effect upon their judgment, not of literary works only, but of men and events in general. They are like persons who have had a very weighty and impressive experience; they are more truly than others under the empire of facts, and more independent of the language current among those with whom they live. They wish neither to applaud nor to revile their age; they wish to know what it is, what it can give them, and whether this is what they want. What they want, they know very well; they want to educe and cultivate what is best and noblest in themselves; they know, too, that this is no easy task—χαλεπὸν, as Pittacus said, χαλεπὸν ἐσθλὸν ἔμμεναι—and they ask themselves sincerely whether their age and its literature can assist them in the attempt. If they are endeavouring to practise any art, they remember the plain and simple proceedings of the old artists, who attained their grand results by penetrating themselves with some noble and significant action, not by inflating themselves with a belief in the preeminent importance and greatness of their own times. They do not talk of their mission, nor of interpreting their age, nor of the coming poet; all this, they know, is the mere delirium of vanity; their business is not to praise their age, but to afford to the men who live in it the highest pleasure which they are capable of feeling. If asked to afford this by means of subjects drawn from the age itself, they ask what special fitness the present age has for supplying them. They are told that it is an era of progress, an age commissioned to carry out the great ideas of industrial development and social amelioration. They reply that with all this they can do nothing; that the elements they need for the exercise of their art are great actions, calculated powerfully and delightfully to affect what is permanent in the human soul; that so far as the present age can supply such actions, they will gladly make use of them; but that an age wanting in moral grandeur can with difficulty supply such, and an age of spiritual discomfort with difficulty be powerfully and delightfully affected by them.

A host of voices will indignantly rejoin that the present age is inferior to the past neither in moral grandeur nor in spiritual health. He who possesses the discipline I speak of will content himself with remembering the judgments passed upon the present age, in this respect, by the men of strongest head and widest culture whom it has produced; by Goethe and by Niebuhr. It will be sufficient for him that he knows the opinions held by these two great men respecting the present age and its literature; and that he feels assured in his own mind that their aims and demands upon life were such as he would wish, at any rate, his own to be; and their judgment as to what is impeding and disabling such as he may safely follow. He will not, however, maintain a hostile attitude towards the false pretensions of his age; he will content himself with not being overwhelmed by them. He will esteem himself fortunate if he can succeed in banishing from his mind all feelings of contradiction, and irritation, and impatience; in order to delight himself with the contemplation of some noble action of a heroic time, and to enable others, through his representation of it, to delight in it also.

I am far indeed from making any claim, for myself

that I possess this discipline ; or for the following poems, that they breathe its spirit. But I say, that in the sincere endeavour to learn and practise, amid the bewildering confusion of our times, what is sound and true in poetical art, I seemed to myself to find the only sure guidance, the only solid footing, among the ancients. They, at any rate, knew what they wanted in art, and we do not. It is this uncertainty which is disheartening, and not hostile criticism. How often have I felt this when reading words of disparagement or of cavil: that it is the uncertainty as to what is really to be aimed at which makes our difficulty, not the dissatisfaction of the critic, who himself suffers from the same uncertainty ! *Non me tua fervida terrent Dicta ;* . . . *Dii me terrent, et Jupiter hostis.*

Two kinds of *dilettanti*, says Goethe, there are in poetry : he who neglects the indispensable mechanical part, and thinks he has done enough if he shows spirituality and feeling; and he who seeks to arrive at poetry merely by mechanism, in which he can acquire an artisan's readiness, and is without soul and matter. And he adds, that the first does most harm to art, and the last to himself. If we must be *dilettanti* : if it is impossible for us, under the circumstances amidst which we live, to think clearly, to feel nobly, and to delineate firmly : if we cannot attain to the mastery of the great artists ;—let us, at least, have so much respect for our art as to prefer it to ourselves. Let us not bewilder our successors ; let us transmit to them the practice of poetry, with its boundaries and wholesome regulative laws, under which excellent works may again, perhaps, at some future time, be produced, not yet fallen into oblivion through our neglect, not yet condemned and cancelled by the influence of their eternal enemy, caprice.

PREFACE TO SECOND EDITION OF POEMS. (1854.)

I HAVE allowed the Preface to the former edition of these Poems to stand almost without change, because I still believe it to be, in the main, true. I must not, however, be supposed insensible to the force of much that has been alleged against portions of it, or unaware that it contains many things incompletely stated, many things which need limitation. It leaves, too, untouched the question, how far and in what manner the opinions there expressed respecting the choice of subjects apply to lyric poetry,—that region of the poetical field which is chiefly cultivated at present. But neither do I propose at the present time to supply these deficiencies, nor, indeed, would this be the proper place for attempting it. On one or two points alone I wish to offer, in the briefest possible way, some explanation.

An objection has been warmly urged to the classing together, as subjects equally belonging to a past time, Œdipus and Macbeth. And it is no doubt true that to

Shakespeare, standing on the verge of the middle ages, the epoch of Macbeth was more familiar than that of Œdipus. But I was speaking of actions as they presented themselves to us moderns: and it will hardly be said that the European mind, in our day, has much more affinity with the times of Macbeth than with those of Œdipus. As moderns, it seems to me, we have no longer any direct affinity with the circumstances and feelings of either. As individuals, we are attracted towards this or that personage, we have a capacity for imagining him, irrespective of his times, solely according to a law of personal sympathy; and those subjects for which we feel this personal attraction most strongly, we may hope to treat successfully. Prometheus or Joan of Arc, Charlemagne or Agamemnon,—one of these is not really nearer to us now than another. Each can be made present only by an act of poetic imagination; but this man's imagination has an affinity for one of them, and that man's for another.

It has been said that I wish to limit the poet, in his choice of subjects, to the period of Greek and Roman antiquity; but it is not so. I only counsel him to choose for his subjects great actions, without regarding to what time they belong. Nor do I deny that the poetic faculty can and does manifest itself in treating the most trifling action, the most hopeless subject. But it is a pity that power should be wasted; and that the poet should be compelled to impart interest and force to his subject, instead of receiving them from it, and thereby doubling his impressiveness. There is, it has been excellently said, an immortal strength in the stories of great actions; the most gifted poet, then, may well be glad to supplement with it that mortal weakness, which, in presence of the vast spectacle of life and the world, he must for ever feel to be his individual portion.

Again, with respect to the study of the classical writers of antiquity; it has been said that we should emulate rather than imitate them. I make no objection; all I say is, let us study them. They can help to cure us of what is, it seems to me, the great vice of our intellect, manifesting itself in our incredible vagaries in literature, in art, in religion, in morals: namely, that it is *fantastic*, and wants *sanity*. Sanity,—that is the great virtue of the ancient literature; the want of that is the great defect of the modern, in spite of all its variety and power. It is impossible to read carefully the great ancients, without losing something of our caprice and eccentricity; and to emulate them we must at least read them.

www.ingramcontent.com/pod-product-compliance
Lightning Source LLC
Chambersburg PA
CBHW030746230426
43667CB00007B/867